Having Your Own Say

Getting the Right Care When It Matters Most

Edited by BERNARD J. HAMMES, PhD
GUNDERSEN HEALTH SYSTEM

INTRODUCTIONS WRITTEN BY SENATOR MARK R. WARNER
AND FORMER GOVERNOR AND SECRETARY MICHAEL LEAVITT

CHT
PRESS
WASHINGTON, DC

Published by CHT Press
1425 K Street NW
Suite 450
Washington, DC 20005
www.healthtransformation.net

President and CEO: Nancy Desmond

Publisher's Cataloging-in-Publication Data

> Having your own say : getting the right care when it matters most / edited by Bernard J. Hammes. – Washington, DC : CHT Press, 2012.
>
> p. ; cm.
>
> ISBN13: 978-1-933966-01-4
>
> 1. Advance directives (Medical care)—United States. 2. Terminal care—United States. 3. Patient advocacy—United States. I. Title. II. Hammes, Bernard J.
>
> R726.2.H38 2012
> 362.175—dc22   2011945113

FIRST EDITION

Project coordination by Jenkins Group, Inc.
www.BookPublishing.com

Cover design by Chris Rhoads
Interior design by Brooke Camfield

Additional copies of this book may be ordered by calling 202-375-2001 or from the CHT website at www.healthtransformation.net.

The authors, editors and publisher of this work have checked with sources believed to be reliable in their efforts to confirm the accuracy and completeness of the information presented. However, neither the authors nor the publisher nor any party involved in the creation and publication of this work warrant that the information is in every respect accurate and complete, and they are not responsible for any errors or omissions or for any consequences from application of the information in this book.

Information provided in this book is for educational and demonstration purposes and is not intended to constitute legal advice. If legal advice is required, the services of a competent professional should be sought. All comments, opinions and observations are those of the authors, and do not represent official positions or opinions unless specifically noted.

Printed in the United States of America
16   15   14   13   12   •   5   4   3   2   1

Advance Praise for *Having Your Own Say*

"*Having Your Own Say* is an eloquent guide from the pioneers who are leading us all on a more humane, sensitive, and sensible path through the final journey of life."

—Ellen Goodman, *Washington Post* longtime syndicated columnist

"When a loved one is seriously ill, our fragmented and impersonal health care system often fails to offer the kind of care we all would want. This important volume shows that there is a better way. I recommend it for everyone who believes, as I do, that we can do better in caring for those with advanced illnesses, and that we can afford to do this if we do it right."

—John Rother, president and CEO,
National Coalition on Health Care

"There are few issues facing our country, our economy, our health care system, and our families that are more pressing than this one. We must take bold and decisive action to prepare ourselves to face this future – our futures – by doing what works, empowering the public, educating health professionals, and creating policy change. This book presents a blueprint for success that should be heeded."

—Nancy Brown, CEO, American Heart Association, and co-chairman,
Coalition to Transform Advanced Care Steering Committee

"As the original provider of patient-centered, palliative care, hospice providers have found that high-quality care – delivered in all settings – begins with a conversation with the patient and their loved ones. This collection of articles demonstrates the essential character of knowing and then honoring the goals and desires of the patient as we provide interdisciplinary care that treats the whole person and not just the illness."

—Don Schumacher, president and CEO,
National Hospice and Palliative Care Organization

Contents

Foreword   ix

   Tom Koutsoumpas and Bill Novelli, codirectors of the Coalition
   to Transform Advanced Care (C-TAC)

Acknowledgments   xix

Introductions   xxi

Moving from Fear to Dialogue

   United States Senator Mark R. Warner, Commonwealth of Virginia

Decisions Should Be Made by Patients and Families, Not by the Government

   Michael Leavitt, Former secretary, Department of Health and Human
   Services, Former Environmental Protection Agency administrator,
   Former governor of Utah, Founder and chairman, Leavitt Partners

Section I   *Putting the Patient and Family*
                   at the Center of the Care Model

One   Putting the Patient and Family at the Center of the Care Model:
      Why We Did It . . . The Value of Care Planning to Our Patients
      and Their Families   5

   Jeff Thompson, MD, chief executive officer, Gundersen Health System

Two   Creating Person-Centered Care When It Matters Most:
      Lessons Learned at Gundersen Health System   11

   Bernard J. Hammes, PhD, director for Respecting Choices and clinical
   ethicist, Gundersen Health System

Three   Helping Individuals Make Informed Healthcare Decisions:
         The Role of the Advance Care Planning Facilitator   23

    Linda A. Briggs, MS, MA, RN, associate director for Respecting Choices
    and ethics consultant, Gundersen Health System

Four   Honoring Choices Minnesota: A Metropolitan
        Program Underway   41

    Kent S. Wilson, MD, medical director, Honoring Choices Minnesota

    Sue A. Schettle, chief executive officer, Twin Cities Medical Society,
    and project director, Honoring Choices Minnesota

Five   Respecting Patient Choices: Scaling Care Planning
        to a Whole Country   57

    William Silvester, MD, national director of the Respecting Patient Choices
    program in Australia and president of the International Society of
    Advance Care Planning and End of Life Care

Section II   *More Care and Support Lead
                 to Better Decisions*

Six   The Value of Palliative Care to Patient and Family Outcomes   71

    R. Sean Morrison, MD, director of the National Palliative Care Research
    Center and vice chair of research and professor of geriatrics and medicine,
    Mount Sinai School of Medicine

    Diane E. Meier, MD, director of the Center to Advance Palliative Care and
    professor of geriatrics and internal medicine and director of the Hertzberg
    Palliative Care Institute, Mount Sinai School of Medicine

Seven   Hope for the Future with a Human Touch:
        Advanced Disease Coordination   87

    Thomas Klemond, MD, practicing palliative physician and medical
    director of Palliative Care and Advanced Disease Coordination Services,
    Gundersen Health System

Eight   Advanced Care: Choice, Comfort, and Control
        for the Seriously Ill   99

    Brad Stuart, MD, chief medical officer, Sutter Care at Home

Nine   Impact of Health Plan Management of Advanced Illness:
The Aetna Compassionate Care Program   123

Randall Krakauer, MD, MBA, national medical director,
Consumer Segment, Aetna

Wayne Rawlins, MD, MBA, national medical director,
Racial and Ethnic Equality Initiatives, Aetna

Ten   Focusing on the Patient's Needs and Desires:
Care at Home   133

Michael Fleming, MD, chief medical officer, Amedisys

Section III   *Perspectives of Persons Receiving Care*

Eleven   The Value of Advance Care Planning:
Perspectives from Patients and Families   149

A Critical Conversation, as told by Jeff Lokken

One of the Most Important Conversations We Had, as told
by Greg Loomis

An Eye-Opening Experience, as told by Arlene Schumacher

Realizing the Importance of Planning Ahead, as told by Evie Herold

A Rainbow of Support, as told by Ruth Nixon Davy

Twelve   How Do Older People and Their Families Benefit
from Advance Care Planning and Support?   161

Naomi Karp, JD, and *Lynn Friss Feinberg, MSW,* senior strategic policy
advisors at the AARP Public Policy Institute

Section IV   *Where's the Money?*

Thirteen   Variation in Health Services Utilization at the End of Life:
A Summary of the Evidence   187

William Brinson Weeks, MD, MBA, associate professor and core faculty
at the Dartmouth Institute for Health Policy and Clinical Practice
and medical director of the High Value Healthcare Collaborative
and the Office of Professional Education and Outreach

Fourteen   "The Right Care, Right Here": How a Palliative Service
            Made Things Better for Patients   201

    Kyla R. Lee, MD, FACP, internal medicine physician, founding member of
    Gundersen Health System's Palliative Care Hospitalist Team, and director
    of the Internal Medicine Clerkship, Gundersen Health System

Fifteen   Better Care, Higher Quality, and Lower Costs
            for the Seriously Ill   211

    Diane E. Meier, MD, and *R. Sean Morrison, MD*

Section V   *What's Next?*

Sixteen   Call to Action: What Needs to Change to Improve Care
            and Allow Sustainability   231

    Jeff Thompson, MD, and *Patrick Fry,* president and chief executive officer,
    Sutter Health

About Gundersen Health System   236

Foreword

NEARLY EVERYONE HAS a personal story about a loved one with an advanced illness. Many of these stories are about the frustrations of dealing with a healthcare system that doesn't truly serve our needs. Patients and their caregivers often are not asked what care they want and are not given options to make good decisions. Instead, they get the care that providers deem best. Research shows that this frequently creates physical, emotional, and financial hardships on patients, families, and caregivers. We are two people with personal stories.

First, Tom Koutsoumpas: *Another trip to the emergency room in the middle of a frigid night was not what Mom wanted, nor was it what my sister, Melinda, and I wanted for her. Our mother was a proud woman who had lived independently for years with multiple chronic conditions. However, she was 85 years old and frail, and, on this night, she had the symptoms of a mild stroke, so what else could we do? This was a recurring cycle over many years. Late at night, when the doctor's office closed, simple answers to simple questions did not come quickly but were rather discovered only after putting Mom through tiresome rounds of ER protocol (CT and MRI scans and countless forms to fill out). Finding answers during "business hours" wasn't much easier. Communication among the numerous specialists treating Mom was seriously lacking. Although I had worked in healthcare for almost all my life and Mom's doctor was a trusted family friend, we felt wholly unprepared, distressed, and lost—until Mom enrolled in hospice care. The hospice team worked with us to coordinate Mom's care and gave her the quality of life, respect, and dignity she deserved.*

Now Bill Novelli: *My brother called while my wife and I were at a memorial service for my mother-in-law in Montana. Our father had suffered a stroke. He was transferred from one hospital to another, and the doctors there said that Dad should be put into an intensive care unit immediately. They might be able to stop the bleeding and stabilize him. We agreed that this wasn't what he told us he wanted, but how could we pass up a chance to save his life? What should we have done? We went along with the doctors' advice. After a very difficult, torturous week, it was clear that he wasn't going to get better. Two hours after we set up a hospice care arrangement (a team came in from outside the hospital), Dad died.*

It doesn't have to be like this. As you will see in the following chapters of this remarkable book, innovative models are emerging that improve the care and personal planning for people like our parents, as well as the millions of other Americans who face advanced illness.

While anyone, even children, can have advanced illness, it disproportionately affects the elderly. In defining the term, we say "advanced illness" occurs when one or more conditions become serious enough that general health and functioning decline, treatment begins to lose its effect, and quality of life increasingly becomes the focus of care. This process continues to the end of life. Uncertainty about prognosis and responsiveness to treatment may require an evolving blend of "curative" interventions to try to beat back the illness's progression and "comfort" (palliative) care to mitigate pain and suffering. Too frequently, however, in the current healthcare system patients and their families face a false dichotomy of choosing either curative care or comfort care. And sometimes the curative care is inappropriate.

Healthcare technology is advancing rapidly, and our physicians, nurses, and other clinicians are trained and equipped to do wonderful things. But the *system for delivering care* has fallen far behind all this. Our healthcare is provided in separate, loosely affiliated silos, whether in hospitals (which provide high-tech, curative treatment), in physician offices and clinics (which address acute complaints), in long-term care facilities (which provide rehabilitation and/or skilled nursing), or in the many other settings where Americans receive healthcare.

In times of serious illness, patients and their families and caregivers are forced to navigate through this maze during an emotionally charged time of life, when outcomes are unclear and support—from spiritual to financial—is needed.

No matter who we are, no matter how knowledgeable or experienced or educated, we need help at times like this. One of our most important challenges, according to a recent survey, is financial.[1] The cost of treatment of a seriously ill family member ranked as the highest concern of Americans. This finding—which trumped concerns of being a burden or not being prepared spiritually for dying—came as a surprise to many in the policy world.

But it isn't really new, and there is a major cause for concern. Back in 1994, a study showed that 31% of families with a loved one struggling with advanced illness lose their savings each year because of the costs of care.[2] Younger families are particularly vulnerable; 43% deplete their savings. The personal and family burdens of out-of-pocket expenses can get lost in debates among policy makers, providers, and others about the costs of advanced illness to the healthcare system.

Although fragmented care and high costs have been the norm until now, things may finally be changing. Innovative models of care have shown that patients and their families can get the higher-quality care they need, with greater patient and family satisfaction and lower costs.

These new models move the focus of care out of the hospital and into patients' homes and communities. No longer are the seriously ill forced to come to their providers. Their providers bring care to them by promoting teamwork, close communication, increased self-confidence, and better self-management. These care teams anticipate problems, work to avoid crises, and often prevent unnecessary hospitalization.

Although these models serve a broader population not yet eligible for hospice, they incorporate the central character of what has been the heart of this nation's hospice philosophy: that knowing and honoring the goals and desires of the patient in the provision of interdisciplinary care are the marks of quality care. Reflected in these new advanced illness models is that gold standard of person-centered palliative care that hospice has provided for decades—giving patients and families the quality, compassionate care that they want. By drawing on the best practices of hospice and other providers, these new models provide better care for our most vulnerable patients.

None of this is about rationing care and deciding who should be treated and who should not. It is not about death panels or "pulling the plug." On the contrary, this is about giving people the care they want, when and where they want it; empowering patients and their families; and preventing unproductive medical interventions that patients do not choose to undergo.

Until now, America has not cared well for people and families struggling with advanced illness, but now we have a way forward: to build on innovative models that actually work. And there is no time to lose. The largest population cohort in American history—the boomers—is coming into its later years. The oldest of the boomers turned 65 this year. This marks the beginning of a long period during which millions of older boomers will draw more and more on the health system as they age.

Many boomers face a dual challenge: caring for their elderly parents and, as time passes, grappling with their own mortality. They are unlikely to do this quietly and without a fuss. Boomers are a feisty generation, and they are going to want clear information, frank discussion, and shared decision making about what comes next, just as they already have throughout each stage of their lives.

So *now* is the time to reform advanced illness care in America, but what is the right vehicle to make it happen? We pondered this question, and so have many others. As a result, a number of us—both individuals and organizations—have come together to form a national, nonprofit, nonpartisan alliance, the Coalition to Transform Advanced Care (C-TAC), which is funded in part by grants from the Peter G. Peterson Foundation and the SCAN Foundation.

In the past year, our coalition has grown to include major health systems, large medical and nursing groups, national consumer organizations, health insurance companies, members of the faith-based community, and hospice and palliative care organizations. The American Academy of Nursing is involved, and so are AARP, Aetna, the American Cancer Society, Ascension Health, the Institute of Medicine, Amedisys, Vanguard Health Systems, the National Hospice and Palliative Care Organization, America's Health Insurance Plans, Gundersen Health System, Sutter Health, the American Heart Association, and many others.

Our purpose is to achieve a true transformation so that *all Americans with advanced illness, especially the sickest and most vulnerable, will receive comprehensive, high-quality, patient-centered care that is consistent with their goals and values and that honors their dignity.*

We recognize that this will take time, resources, and hard work. But we also know that it can and must be done. Those millions of boomers are a powerful reason why. So is the national debate over America's debt and deficit. We can't rein in our huge debt without controlling soaring healthcare expenditures. Research shows that giving people quality advanced illness care can improve patient and family satisfaction and simultaneously provide cost reductions that far outweigh the initial investments.

Many of the contributors to this book are involved in C-TAC and are focused on four key integrated areas:

- Do what works: promote best-practice care delivery (the models that work in clinical and community settings) to ensure high-quality, coordinated advanced illness care, across all settings;
- Empower the public: help people to understand and make informed choices for themselves and their families and to call for change in care delivery and in policies;
- Educate health professionals: to better serve patients and families/ caregivers so people know their options, make informed choices, get the care they need, and avoid procedures they don't want;

- Create policy change: develop and advocate for federal and state legislative, regulatory, judicial, and administrative initiatives and also for private policies, to improve care for those with advanced illness.

This book leads the way forward. It contains the newest thinking and proven solutions to long-standing, difficult problems in advanced illness and end-of-life care. The path to successful reform lies in getting every one of us involved. We welcome the participation of organizations and individuals committed to achieving high-quality, person-centered care for people with advanced illness. Let's not let this opportunity pass us by. And let's share our personal stories and make the most of what we learn together.

Tom Koutsoumpas is executive director of the Mintz Levin Center for Health Law and Policy and senior vice president of ML Strategies/U.S., the consulting division of the Mintz Levin law firm. Mr. Koutsoumpas also cofounded and now cochairs the Coalition to Transform Advanced Care (C-TAC). C-TAC is a national, nonprofit, nonpartisan alliance of patient and consumer advocacy groups, healthcare professionals and providers, private-sector stakeholders, faith-based organizations, and healthcare payers with the shared mission to help provide all Americans, especially the sickest and most vulnerable, with comprehensive, high-quality, patient-centered care that is consistent with their goals and values and honors their dignity.

Mr. Koutsoumpas has more than 35 years of experience in government, public policy, and issue advocacy at the federal and state levels.

Before joining Mintz Levin, he served as corporate vice president with UnitedHealth Group, where he oversaw the organization's federal government affairs. Prior to his work with UnitedHealth Group, he was executive vice president and chief of public affairs at VITAS Healthcare Corporation, the nation's largest provider of hospice and palliative care. While serving as executive vice president, he was a member of the senior management team. His work experience prior to that includes serving as senior advisor and executive assistant to former Indiana Governor and Senator Evan Bayh; working in health policy as a member of the health practice group of Hogan and Hartson law firm (now Hogan Lovells); and serving as an associate in public affairs for Burson Marsteller, one of the nation's largest public relations firms. Initially, he began his career in public policy and worked in the U.S. Senate for Senator Birch Bayh for more than 11 years while serving in numerous legislative and staff capacities.

Mr. Koutsoumpas serves on the Board of Directors of the National Hospice Foundation, an organization committed to promoting compassionate care at the end of life. He also serves on the board of the National Coalition for Cancer Survivorship (NCCS) and was recently appointed chair-elect. NCCS is the oldest survivor-led cancer advocacy group in the country and is dedicated to advocating for quality cancer care for all Americans and empowering cancer survivors. He serves on the transitional Board of Directors of the National Center for Medical-Legal Partnership (MLP), a growing nonprofit organization that provides technical and informational support for medical-legal partnership programs in hundreds of hospitals and health centers across America. Most recently, he was elected to serve on the board of Capital Caring Inc. Capital Caring is a leading provider of hospice and palliative care to those living with serious illness in the Washington metropolitan area. Tom has been a member of the Business-Government Relations Council in Washington, DC, and a former member of the Board of Regents of Georgetown University.

Mr. Koutsoumpas is a graduate of Georgetown University with a degree in American studies.

Bill Novelli is a professor in the McDonough School of Business at Georgetown University. In addition to teaching in the MBA program, he is working to establish a center for social enterprise at the school. From 2001 to 2009, he was CEO of AARP, a membership organization of more than 40 million people 50 and older. During his tenure, the organization achieved important policy successes at national and state levels in health, financial security, good government, and other areas. It also doubled its budget, added five million new members, and expanded internationally.

Prior to joining AARP, Mr. Novelli was president of the Campaign for Tobacco-Free Kids, whose mandate is to change public policies and the social environment, limit tobacco companies' marketing and sales practices to children, and serve as a counterforce to the tobacco industry and its special interests. He now serves as chairman of the board.

Previously, he was executive vice president of CARE, the world's largest private relief and development organization. He was responsible for all operations in the United States and abroad. CARE helps impoverished people in Africa, Asia, and Latin America through programs in health, agriculture, environmental protection, and small-business support. CARE also provides emergency relief to people in need.

Earlier, Mr. Novelli cofounded and was president of Porter Novelli, now one of the world's largest public relations agencies and part of the Omnicom Group, an international marketing communications corporation. He directed numerous corporate accounts as well as the management and development of the firm. Porter Novelli was founded to apply marketing to social and health issues and grew into an international marketing/public relations agency with corporate, not-for-profit, and government clients. He retired from the firm in 1990 to pursue a second career in public service. He was named one of the 100 most influential public relations professionals of the twentieth century by the industry's leading publication.

Mr. Novelli is a recognized leader in social marketing and social change and has managed programs in cancer control, diet and nutrition, cardiovascular health, reproductive health, infant survival, pay increases for educators, charitable giving, and other programs in the United States and the developing world.

References

1. Living well at the end of life: a national conversation. *National Journal* Web site. http:// syndication.nationaljournal.com/communications/ NationalJournalRegenceToplines.pdf. Accessed August 26, 2011.

2. The SUPPORT Investigators. A controlled trial to improve care for seriously ill hospitalized patients: the study to understand prognoses and preferences for outcomes and risks of treatments (SUPPORT). *JAMA: Journal of the American Medical Association.* 1995;274(20):1591-1598.

Acknowledgments

THIS BOOK WOULD not have been possible without the help of many people. Cathy L. Fischer, a writer and editor at Gundersen Health System, worked long and diligently to review each and every section of the book and made sure that it all worked together. Janelle Roghair, a writer from Gundersen Health System, also needs to be recognized for her efforts to work with the patients and families to tell their stories. And last, but not least, the patients and family members who shared their stories in this book need to be particularly recognized. Their willingness to share their private stories with readers is a great gift that is both inspirational and insightful.

This book is dedicated to the health professionals and the patients of the La Crosse community.

Introductions

Moving from Fear to Dialogue

—United States Senator Mark R. Warner

"**DYING IS AT** once a fact of life and a profound mystery."

Those were the opening words of a 1997 Institute of Medicine report[1] that sought to explain what Americans knew about healthcare at the end of life and to offer recommendations to knock down barriers to good care. Since then, we have seen some growth in the thinking on these issues. However, families are still often left alone to grapple with extraordinarily difficult decisions about how to care for those with advanced illness. Doctors are often unsure about their patients' wishes. And patients end up facing a needlessly limited set of options.

I know firsthand just how tough this can be on patients and their families. My mom suffered from Alzheimer's disease for 10 years before her death in January 2010. When she was first diagnosed more than a decade ago, my family didn't really take the opportunity to talk in a frank and fully informed way with her and her healthcare providers about the full array of care options. We did not discuss living wills, advance directives, or what her priorities would be during the final years of her life.

I was an informed citizen at the time, the governor of Virginia, and yet my family and I did not have a full understanding of all that could be before us. With more information and support, we could have held important family discussions with my mother and worked with her doctors and pastor to craft a care plan that truly reflected her wishes.

We all understand why these conversations inspire anxiety. Death often remains beyond our comprehension; the impending loss of a loved one is frightening. Too often, misinformation makes the topic difficult to confront in the public policy debate.

We certainly saw that during the 2009 healthcare reform debate when proposals to allow physician reimbursement for counseling seniors about advance directives were labeled as calls for "death panels." In fact, the mere mention of improving "end-of-life care" led to public denunciations, as though there were some plot to deny critical care to our loved ones.

In truth, these conversations and policy discussions are really about the quality of aging and not about limiting anyone's healthcare. My mother's story is not unique, and my family is certainly not alone in having difficulty discussing these sensitive advanced care issues without support.

As scary as it may be, we must be honest about care options, treatment settings, and the planning that may dramatically improve the quality of life of patients and their family caregivers.

This book highlights a different story, one in which practitioners, patients, and families are given the ability to choose another way—a better way—to provide care to loved ones during the closing chapters of life. Across the country, people are innovating and creating new models of care that put patients and their caregivers at the center of this decision making, giving all people more care and support and better tools to make the decisions that are right for them.

Informed, honest discussions are more critical than ever as the vast "baby boom" generation ages into Medicare. The number of Americans eligible for Medicare will grow at a rate of about 3% per year. That's a million and half new beneficiaries each year between 2011 and 2020.

Medicare spends nearly 30% of its budget on beneficiaries in their final year of life, and slightly more than half of Medicare dollars are spent on patients who ultimately die within two months.

Current payment models actually discourage coordination among providers during these last months and years. Our existing system rewards overutilization rather than reimbursing medical professionals for conversations and planning on what a patient might truly want or what better reflects his or her values.

Ample research has shown that providing comprehensive, patient-centered care leads to better quality, greater patient satisfaction, and lower costs. We know this, so we should act on it. This also means expanding, not limiting, choice.

I am thrilled that this distinguished group of people has come together to tell the story of how they have worked to transform the culture in their communities to change the way to provide advanced care. As you read, take note of these innovative programs that have produced increased satisfaction from patients and families while maintaining or improving quality and lowering costs to patients and the healthcare system as a whole.

These stories can help us pave a way for smarter payment models and better care systems nationwide. It is possible to put the focus on continuous, coordinated, and comprehensive care regardless of the setting. It is possible to give patients and their caregivers autonomy to make informed choices. And it is critically important that we design and implement support systems that approach these issues for individuals with advanced illness in a more holistic and empowering way.

This country has an amazing healthcare system that is enabling us to live longer than ever before. We need to ensure that we also have a healthcare system that enables us to make affirmative, personal decisions about the quality of our lives when illness becomes advanced. Through an open, honest discussion, we can begin to develop a culture in which all of us will have the ability to age well, with dignity, in the setting of our choosing, knowing that our wishes will be respected.

Reference

1.   Institute of Medicine. *Approaching death: improving care at the end of life.* Washington, DC: National Academy Press; 1997:1.

Decisions Should Be Made by Patients and Families, Not by the Government

—Michael Leavitt

RECENTLY, MY WIFE and I sat with our legal adviser to make a long-overdue review of our wills. A lot has changed since we sat, as a younger couple, to make plans our optimism told us would never be used.

Gratefully, Jackie and I are both in excellent health, but the most sobering part of the discussion came when we reached the part of the document titled "Advance Directives." It dealt with the difficult-to-contemplate situations that occur when a person is seriously ill but incapable of making his or her own decisions. Over the years, I have been close to several situations where this occurred and have come to know well the benefit to loved ones when people have made their wishes known.

As secretary of Health and Human Services, I came to understand that while this type of decision making is uncomfortable for all of us, it is even more challenging if we leave it to others—either our family or society. In fact, these decisions are the granddaddy of political hot potatoes. The faintest whiff of such decisions being addressed in public policy inspires unfortunate political phrases such as "death panels." As a result, political leaders don't talk about them much.

Our nation's escalating deficit and debt are well chronicled. Medicare and Medicaid spending is at the heart of the problem. Nearly a third of all Medicare spending occurs in the last 30 days of life. The mounting cost of Medicare looms as a daunting fiscal monster that, if left unresolved, will make constraining costs a near-impossible political task.

Despite the mounting cost of Medicare, the treatment decisions of patients need to be left to these patients, their families, and the health professionals who provide the care rather than to the government. This is a personal responsibility we must all shoulder voluntarily. My worry is that if too few of us make the decisions voluntarily, someday government officials, with their backs to the financial wall, will feel that they have no alternative but to begin making decisions about the care that people with advanced illness will and will not receive. It happens in other countries now.

People with advanced illness should be encouraged to do voluntary advance care planning and be offered expanded care options. An important step forward would be for medical payers (insurance companies, Medicare, and Medicaid) to compensate health professionals who provide voluntary advance care planning and to provide a wider range of support services for patients with advanced illness as described in this book. The result will be improved patient and family satisfaction, no government involvement in deeply personal decisions, and lower healthcare costs.

Let me illustrate why this is so important by relating two experiences of a surgeon friend of mine.

The first experience involved a woman in her mid-70s whose colon cancer had metastasized to her lungs and liver. While examining her, the surgeon found a perforated ulcer that he believed was the result of multiple rounds of chemotherapy. She confided in him that her oncologist continued to recommend chemotherapy treatments even though she was not sure whether they were extending her life. In fact, the patient knew her time was limited but wanted to go on a couple of family trips, and she did not want another round of chemotherapy and the associated loss of hair.

Surgeons are paid when they operate; oncologists are paid when they provide chemotherapy. They are not compensated to spend hours helping patients make one of the most important medical decisions of their lives. However, in this case, the surgeon—without compensation—helped the patient, her family, and her oncologist develop a plan. They got her discharged from the hospital and introduced her to hospice. They were able to control her pain and avoid additional chemotherapy. She kept her hair and completed the family trips before she passed.

The second case involved a woman in her late 80s who was admitted to the hospital with failing health. During her hospital stay, she developed a bleeding ulcer. She faced a dilemma. Without surgery, she would bleed to death, but her capacity to survive the surgery was doubtful. If she survived the surgery, her life quality would suffer. Doctors advised the family to consider "comfort care" rather than pursuing surgery. Her adult children felt that this was the right decision, but her husband wanted "everything done."

Understandably, the family deferred to their grieving father. The surgery successfully stopped the bleeding, but her health continued to fail. She died in the hospital after approximately eight expensive weeks of intensive care from complications related to the surgery.

These two families chose different treatment approaches. Neither involved government coercion. Both families made informed decisions. Both got the care they requested. One patient's self-interested decision prevented a six-figure medical bill for taxpayers. She didn't need the government to help her, but she did need her doctor to help her and a different, palliative approach of care to support her choice.

When people know the facts, they make good decisions. Without good advice and a wider set of choices, everything in the system leads people to the most expensive—and often inhuman—pathway of care.

In this book, the contributing authors describe how the health system might be reorganized so that patients and families both can make informed, voluntary choices about the care that will best serve them when faced with advanced illness and can get the healthcare services that most meet these preferences and goals. This new model has been demonstrated in different parts of the country and with different populations of patients. If this model of care can be generalized and made the standard throughout the United States, we could accomplish an important public policy goal: honoring individual choices, controlling cost without limiting choices, and keeping the government out of making these decisions for us.

If left to society, this is an agonizingly difficult problem. However, when Jackie and I had finished the conversation with our adviser that day, it was a satisfying feeling to know that our family would be spared the grief of uncertainty. The truth is that no matter what people decide, the outcome is positive. It assures that people receive the care they want, and it spares families untold grief.

This new approach to healthcare is difficult to talk about, but there are humanitarian and economic imperatives that we start. This book gives us a place to begin that conversation. It is now time for all persons, of all political points of view, to use the best knowledge and experience to improve our healthcare system.

Section I

Putting the Patient and Family at
the Center of the Care Model

IN RECENT YEARS, many health leaders and experts have argued that we must make healthcare delivery more "patient centered." Patient-centered care is care of each person on the basis of an individualized understanding of that person. It is difficult to find fault with this goal. We all want our physicians and nurses to know and treat us as individuals rather than solely by some standard protocol.

Putting this goal into practice is challenging, at best. Healthcare these days is delivered by complicated arrangements made up of many different health professionals often working at different health organizations. It is sometimes difficult to communicate correctly about even basic things such as what medications a patient is taking or what tests he or she has had.

Simply telling health professionals that they need to be or should be more patient centered will not result in any significant improvement. Motivating health professionals is really not the issue. Even training health professionals to be more patient centered will not be enough. Improving individual behavior alone will not make a significant impact on the care of a population of patients. Ultimately, healthcare will become more patient centered only when healthcare as a system is redesigned to routinely put the patient's individuality at the center of the care model.

Part I of this book describes how one Midwest health system and one community redesigned the care model to put the individual and his or her family squarely at the center of the model. In chapter 1, Jeff Thompson, MD, chief executive officer of Gundersen Health System, explains why the organization designed new approaches to better understand and honor patient values and preferences. In chapter 2, Bernard J. Hammes, PhD, the clinical ethicist at Gundersen Health System, describes in greater detail how this advance care planning system works and why it is a challenge for other health systems to implement it. Next, in chapter 3, Linda Briggs, MS, MA, RN, a nurse ethicist at Gundersen Health System, explores the crucial importance of advance care planning conversations and describes Gundersen Health System's team approach to interacting with patients to help them make informed plans by using trained advance care planning facilitators. In chapter 4, Kent Wilson, MD, and Sue Schettle, from the Twin Cities Medical Society of Minneapolis/St. Paul, Minnesota, provide a detailed account of how the lessons learned at Gundersen and in La Crosse to promote advance care planning have been scaled up to work in a large, diverse metropolitan area. Finally, in chapter 5, Bill Silvester, MD, a critical care physician from the Austin Medical Center outside Melbourne, Australia, describes how his group took the advance care planning program developed at Gundersen and scaled the program for use throughout a national health system.

It is important to keep in mind as you read these chapters that the advance care planning system developed in La Crosse, called Respecting Choices, is NOT a program to simply complete legal advance directive documents. It is a program to assist patients and their families to make informed decisions about future medical care, to ensure that these plans are well documented and updated over time, and to ensure that they are available to all health professionals who are involved or become involved in the persons' care. This systematic advance care planning approach helps organize an individualized plan of care for each patient that stays with the person from place to place and from provider to provider. It is also something that changes and becomes more specific over time. Ultimately, this work has not only improved our understanding of the individual patient but also helped the providers of healthcare to develop better, more individualized ways to provide care and treatment. Not only is Respecting Choices about having a thoughtful conversation with patients over time; it is also about improving the healthcare delivery model so that individualized plans of care can actually be provided.

one

Putting the Patient and Family at the Center of the Care Model: Why We Did It . . . The Value of Care Planning to Our Patients and Their Families

—Jeff Thompson, MD

WE ALL DIE. A fundamental question is, do we want to have a say in how we live? If that is the case, then it is reasonable that we give others a say in how they would like to live. It is easy to affirm such basic principles; however, the most recent data[1] reveal that a large percentage of individuals, especially those in later years of their life, either have not made clear their wishes or their clear wishes have been lost in an unclear system. For such a critical, basic part of one's existence, it would seem that we would have a better track record.

It's not that it hasn't been noticed. For decades, the topic has been discussed. Presidents and healthcare leaders have made reference to advance care planning or end-of-life coordination of care. In 1991, Congress got into the act and passed the Patient Self-Determination Act, which required healthcare organizations to inform patients of their rights and to ask them about their advance directives upon admission to the hospital. The law's requirements that staff members help provide community education have been even less well implemented than the hospital-focused expectation.

The reasons we have not made greater progress more quickly are many. Healthcare organizations have neither made advance care planning a priority, nor taken it on as a responsibility. Progress has also been hampered by patients and families believing that filling out a document at some point took care of the issue for all time. Finally, for many patients and families, complex legal forms—intimidating and sometimes poorly understood—have been a considerable barrier.

Even if patients had understood and the documents had been well drawn up, there is often no system in place to make the documents readily available, to allow them to be readily used, and to make them the foundation for guiding the patient's care going forward. Further, healthcare workers and community members frequently lack sufficient knowledge and understanding to support patients and families. In addition, on occasion, political dynamics have led to confusion between patient-controlled care and government intervention. For all these reasons, programs have varied widely in terms of effectiveness, engagement of patients and their families, and documented outcomes.

In addition, health professionals have been and continue to be intimately involved and tremendously drained by a lack of clarity around patient wishes and needs. We expend tremendous wealth in talent and technology to provide care that patients may not want or need, leading to moral distress of our staff.

To advance from the current state to a much stronger patient- and family-directed model of care, the health system as a whole must assume responsibility for that change.

In the mid-1980s, Gundersen Health System's clinical ethicist[2] began to conduct ethics consultations as part of his role on the Gundersen Ethics Committee. Over several months, he faced three situations that called for new thinking about how health professionals cared for patients. These cases involved patients with end-stage renal disease who had suffered devastating strokes.

Healthcare providers expected these patients to survive for some time if dialysis was continued, but they did not expect the patients to regain awareness of self, others, or their surroundings. In all three situations, the patients would be physically dependent on others for care and require continued dialysis three times a week. Their loving families did not know what to do. When asked "What would your parent want in this situation?" the families all responded in the same way: "If only we knew!"

In each case, three things were clear: (1) we did not, and never would, know for certain what the patient wanted; (2) no matter what decision they made, the families and health professionals would live with considerable uncertainty about their decision, resulting in lasting distress; and (3) the uncertainty required incredible amounts of staff time while attempting to sort through the ethical complexities. These outcomes were bad for patients, bad for their families, and bad for the health professionals who were caring for them.

The conversations needed to occur early on, when patients and their families would have time to not only discuss the issues but also disseminate the decisions to the multiple healthcare personnel with whom patients may come in contact. Healthcare providers needed to be trained to understand the legal and emotional environment surrounding these documents, and systems had to be developed to support the choices the patients made.

The original trial was in the renal dialysis unit, where it was quickly found that if one engaged the families as well as the patients, if it was done sooner rather than later, if the clinical staff were trained rather than left adrift, and if you had adequate support for both aggressive care and less aggressive care, you could rapidly move from a small number of patients having their wishes understood and carried out to a majority of patients having their wishes understood and carried out.

The keys to early success resulted from the primary focus on the wellbeing of patients and their families. Success was increased by better availability of documentation of the patients' choices and better staff understanding of the patients' desires.

The spread to the community has had a similar focus. Not only have leaders of healthcare institutions been involved but also leaders in schools, religious institutions, and community organizations have contributed staff, time, and their assent to how valuable it is to the fabric of the country. This involvement allowed the community to have these discussions and build a system to follow up on them. Far from the angst sometimes ascribed to this activity as being a controlling mechanism by government or healthcare, these were trained volunteers, parish nurses, and retired school teachers sitting with friends, families, and community members to talk about how patients wanted their lives to be lived. This was nothing about outside control but everything about having patients determine for themselves how they were going to live.

That fundamental principle helped carry this effort past a normal project or program to a community-wide effort that was an understood and accepted part of the health and well-being of our communities. The effort was aided by having health systems willing to invest in combined inpatient and outpatient medical records, which made these documents steadily more available, and in training staff in home care, hospice, and palliative care to provide opportunities if the patient chose a less aggressive approach.

So why we pressed down this path has everything to do with the well-being of patients, their families, and the health professionals who care for them. It is to preemptively answer the question "What would your parent, your spouse, your loved one want in this situation?" The purpose is to avoid anyone needing to say "We wish we knew." With this approach, we have helped tens of thousands of individuals take the opportunity to determine how they are going to live. In his August 2010 *New Yorker* article, Dr. Atul Gawande summed it up this way: "It was that simple—and that complicated."[3]

Jeff Thompson, MD, is chief executive officer and chairman of the Boards of Gundersen Health System and a practicing pediatric intensivist and neonatologist. He is a founding member and past board chair of the Wisconsin Collaborative for Healthcare Quality. Presently, he is chairman of the board of the La Crosse Medical Health Science Consortium.

Dr. Thompson graduated in 1978 from the University of Wisconsin–Madison Medical School. He completed his pediatric internship at the University of California–Davis from 1978 to 1979. He was a pediatric resident and then chief resident from 1979 to 1982 at Upstate Medical Center in Syracuse, New York, and finished his neonatal fellowship in 1984 at that same institution. Dr. Thompson is board certified in pediatric critical care, neonatal and perinatal medicine, and pediatrics. He is a member of the American Academy of Pediatrics, as well as its subsections in neonatal and critical care medicine, and is a member of the American College of Physician Executives. Dr. Thompson has authored many articles, book chapters, and abstracts on many healthcare topics.

Since completing his professional training in 1984, Dr. Thompson has worked full time solely at Gundersen Clinic and Lutheran Hospital–La Crosse (now Gundersen Health System). From 1992 to 1996, he served on the former Board of Directors of Gundersen Clinic and played a key role in the negotiations and governance design that led to the merger between Gundersen Clinic and Lutheran Hospital. Since 1996, Dr. Thompson has been a member of the board of governors and a member of the board of trustees. He served as executive vice president from 1995 to 2001. From 2001 to present he has served as chief executive officer.

References

1. Wenger NS, Shugarman LR, Wilkinson A. Advance directives and advance
    care planning: report to Congress, August 2008. http://aspe.hhs.gov/daltcp/
    reports/2008/adcongrpt.htm. Accessed August 24, 2011.

2. This clinical ethicist is also the editor of this book.

3. Gawande A. Letting go: what should medicine do when it can't save your life? *The
    New Yorker*, August 2, 2010.

two

Creating Person-Centered Care When It Matters Most: Lessons Learned at Gundersen Health System

—Bernard J. Hammes, PhD

LET'S BEGIN WITH a story. This story is neither a feel-good fairy tale nor an entertaining action-thriller. This story is a moral drama that has featured or will likely feature each of us.

The plotline is simple. Having lived with an advanced illness for several years, someone you love dearly is now seriously ill. There are options for treatment, but there is considerable uncertainty about the ending. None of the probable outcomes is attractive. There are serious risks and burdens from attempting the treatments. Even with treatment, your loved one's death in the near future is highly probable. You are asked by the treating physician, "What would your loved one want us to do in this situation?" You realize in a moment of stark clarity that you don't know the answer, but you also know that you cannot avoid making a decision. Whatever you decide will have a profound, lasting effect on the person you love. You also realize that you will never know whether you made the right decision.

This tragic story line is lived out in hundreds of health organizations in the United States every day. It is a story where the patient's chronic illness gets worse and the loved ones suffer with the responsibility to decide. A few of these cases have been played out in our courts and news media, but almost all are faced privately, as bedside dramas, lived by families of all backgrounds, cultures, religious traditions, and races. Just as modern medical technology is part of our life, so, too, is the moral burden of the decision in this story. It is an unavoidable part of the contemporary human experience, and we have struggled to create effective human and social responses to it.

The most widespread social response has been the creation of laws that permit adults to sign documents that specify their preferences for future healthcare decisions. These documents typically fall into two categories: living wills and powers of attorney for healthcare. Living wills are documents that provide only instructions, typically about stopping medical treatment either when you have been determined to be terminally ill (i.e., you will die soon regardless of any treatment) or when you are in a persistent vegetative state (i.e., you lack any awareness but still open your eyes at times and fall asleep at times). Powers of attorney for healthcare are documents that allow you to appoint another person (or series of persons) who would have authority to make your healthcare decisions if you became incapable of making them yourself. In the most recent versions of this type of legislation and effort, these two documents are often combined so that an individual can create a legal document that not only appoints someone to make his or her healthcare decisions when he or she is incapable but also provides instructions about how to make decisions and what decisions to make. All of these documents are typically called advance directives (ADs).

A newer approach to documenting a care plan that is rapidly being adopted in the United States is the Physician Orders for Life-Sustaining Treatment (POLST) paradigm. This paradigm goes by different names in different states, including MOLST, POST, and MOST, as well as POLST. This approach uses a standardized set of medical orders on a single sheet of brightly colored paper that stays with a patient as he or she moves across healthcare settings.[1] The POLST paradigm is designed for those individuals who have advanced illness and whose death in the next 12 months would not be a surprise. The POLST form can be used to order treatments to be provided, not provided, or some combination of both. This POLST paradigm provides a powerful way of creating highly specific care plans that all health professionals caring for a patient can follow, even when that patient needs to be transported from one place to another.[2,3] The POLST paradigm can be far more effective than ADs alone for this population of patients.

While the AD and POLST legislation and regulation have created important tools for documentation, by themselves they do not fully resolve the real, tragic moral dilemmas faced by so many families. These legal responses focus on questions such as which form to use and how to fill out the form rather than the moral and human question "How should we take good care of this person in these circumstances?" So, while we needed clarification on the legal boundaries and processes, these efforts alone are insufficient to fully address the moral/human problem that we face.

One community in La Crosse, Wisconsin, has developed a more comprehensive model to help individuals and their families create personal health plans for these morally complex healthcare decisions. This La Crosse model starts from the assumption that it is necessary to redesign the health system so that, as a matter of routine, it is focused on the person and knowing the values and goals of each person. This approach has come to be called "patient-centered" care. Being focused on the person is not inherently about individual autonomy or legal rights; rather, it is about understanding the views, values, history, and relationships that a person finds important and how these realities should guide medical decisions about the benefits and burdens of medical treatment. The focus on knowing patients as people means that assisting them in care planning starts not with legal documents or forms but, rather, with interactions and conversations.

It means investing in interactions where persons can better understand what choices they need to consider; thoughtfully reflecting on those choices in light of their views, values, and relationships; and, finally, discussing these ideas and plans with those whom they most love. It also means undertaking these conversations in a way and at a pace acceptable to the persons.

Care planning needs to take into account the stage of health or illness of the persons and to plan for what is appropriate or possible at that stage of health. In the La Crosse model, we assist persons and their families in three distinct stages of health: (1) when people are healthy, we promote basic planning that typically creates a power of attorney for healthcare with specific instructions about if and when a severe, permanent brain injury or disease might change the goals of treatment from prolonging life to focusing on comfort; (2) when people have a progressive, advanced illness and begin to experience serious complications from that illness, we do disease-specific planning that provides specific instructions about when a devastating complication from the illness would alter the goals of care; and finally, (3) when we won't be surprised if the people die of their known illness in the next 12 months, we talk in more detail about specific treatment issues that are documented on the POLST form.

Such conversations take considerable time, and health professionals need to develop additional skills and competence to facilitate them well for each stage of the illness. In La Crosse, this reality led to the creation of a new role in healthcare: an advance care planning (ACP) facilitator. These facilitators are typically staff who already have professional skills and who would have the time needed to devote to facilitating these conversations, usually from 30 to 90 minutes. These facilitators work as part of a team that has the patient's physician as the central member.

To be successful, however, this new ACP system had to have more than facilitators. Other roles and responsibilities had to be considered and designed. These staff needed to be instructed on how to play these roles. So from the receptionist in the outpatient clinic to the medical records personnel, from the bedside nurse to the physician in the wellness clinic, each had a unique role to play in the

ACP system. Each role needed to be carefully thought out, and staff needed to be trained and held accountable to play their roles.

In addition, the system needed standardized ways to document not only the interactions with patients but also what plans were created. In the La Crosse community, the health organizations were not satisfied with the power of attorney for healthcare document created in state law, so they created a new state-law-compliant document that was easier to read, easier to fill out, and more comprehensive and clinically useful.[4] This document was designed to complement the conversation process. In addition, the health organizations in La Crosse decided to implement the POLST paradigm. This program provided another specific tool to complement the power of attorney for healthcare for those who were most likely to face serious medical problems. POLST has made an important contribution because it helped guide treatment even as a critically ill person was being transferred from, say, long-term care to an ambulance, to the emergency room, to a hospital bed. The POLST form made it possible for a highly individualized plan to be created and to be followed even in complex transitions of care, whether the plan was for all treatment, comfort care, or anything in between.

Medical record systems were also designed so that care plans were entered and maintained in a patient's medical records in a consistent manner and were always available to providers when needed. In the beginning, care plans were stored in the paper medical record but now are a part of the electronic medical record. Specific staff were made responsible for making sure that any ADs and/ or POLST a patient had were (1) entered into his or her medical record, (2) updated over time, and (3) transferred from one facility to another so they were available to the patient's next physician.

Before these ACP systems were implemented, other local groups were engaged and included in the decision to implement the program. These groups included religious leaders; service groups; members of the county bar association; and public institutions, such as schools and libraries. This engagement was essential to establish trust and widespread support for this work.

To make the promotion of ACP easier and more effective, educational materials using a common name, logo, and messages, including print and video materials, were developed and used as a standard of care by the major health providers in all settings of care. Rather than promoting the mere completion of legal documents, these materials promoted discussions and conversations and provided guidance on when and how to have these conversations.

Finally, all these care planning systems were not only managed over time but also subjected to quality improvement processes so that poorly functioning processes could be identified and improved.

This ACP program in La Crosse is known as Respecting Choices.[5] The systems described above were initially put into place in the La Crosse region from 1991 to 1993. The POLST program was introduced in La Crosse in 1997. Gundersen Health System, in collaboration with the other health organizations in La Crosse, has continued to monitor the outcomes of this system. The latest study data[6] collected in 2007 and 2008 have demonstrated that there is a very high prevalence of care plans for adults who die in health organizations in La Crosse County (90%), that almost all of these care plans are available in the medical record of the health organization where people died (99.4%), and that the treatments provided are consistent with care plans almost all the time (99%). In addition, at the time of death, 67% of individuals also have a POLST form. These documents are almost always in the medical record and are consistently followed. In the 400 consecutive deaths reviewed in all settings of care in La Crosse County, 96% had some type of plan available at the health organization where the patient died.

This is what person-centered care could look like: a community-wide health system that organizes itself so that it makes a concerted, planned effort to talk with patients and those closest to them about their values and their healthcare goals and these personal health plans are recorded and documented so that all health providers not only have access to them but also know how to use them to provide the right treatment to each and every individual. The ultimate goal is to make sure that patients receive just the treatment they want based on truly informed decisions and to avoid over- or undertreatment.

But the value of this approach isn't about only the value of respecting or honoring a patient's values and goals. There are other benefits. These other benefits include (1) avoiding treatments the patient considers burdensome, thus avoiding unnecessary suffering and indignity; (2) being better able to provide care where the person would want it; and (3) diminishing or eliminating the moral distress and its lasting effects experienced by family members who must make healthcare decisions when they do not know what their loved one would want.[7,8]

Finally, there is a potential positive side effect of such care planning that has a benefit for everyone: lowering the cost of care. While neither the aim nor the goal of good care planning, cost savings have been noted in many places where effective care planning has been implemented.[9] Savings come not as a result of denying treatment to any person; rather, savings occur because we know that, from the person's perspective, certain medical interventions are no longer of value to him or her. The vast majority of Americans are very clear about one value: "I don't want to die hooked up to machines." If a person holds this value and documents it in a care plan and if we can honor it almost all of the time, we can eliminate the high cost of medical intervention at the very end AND we can focus our care on the relief of physical, emotional, and spiritual suffering.

In summary, an effective care planning system benefits everyone. It's a more person-centered system of care, so not only can we more thoughtfully tailor medical treatments to the person but also we can avoid unnecessary suffering for that person. We can help relieve families of the nearly impossible moral burden of making difficult healthcare decisions for someone they deeply care about. For the health system, we can bring to bear the vast array of medical services in a way that best carries out the professional responsibility to act in the patient's best interest and to minimize unnecessary suffering. For the payment system, we can avoid using extensive services by making sure that patients receive only those services they desire.

So, if this can be done in La Crosse, why isn't it done everywhere? In some of the chapters that follow, other authors will describe how it is being done elsewhere. But in our current U.S. health system, there are enormous barriers to creating effective care planning systems that are truly person centered.

Perhaps the biggest barrier is the disparity between the costs of implementing and maintaining the care planning system compared with what our current system pays health professionals to provide. Establishing an effective care planning system incurs real costs. Health administrators need to budget for the time to create a care planning system, for the staff to be retrained to play new roles, for medical records processes to be reorganized, and for staff to be provided the time to facilitate the conversation with patients and their families. But in our current payment system, there is little or no reimbursement for all this work. Given this reality, it is understandable why the prevalence of effective care plans remains low and the moral distress described in the opening story line remains common.

Perhaps the second biggest barrier stems from the fact that creating such a person-centered health system requires a huge shift in how we provide health services. Like all human systems or processes, healthcare tends to do what it has done. We have had decades of experience of treating acute medical problems in high-tech facilities such as emergency departments and intensive care units. As a system, we are very good at providing this care and treatment, and this is exactly the care and treatment that many patients need and desire. Clearly, we do not want to undermine this capacity! But as we have gotten better and better at managing progressive, chronic illness and prolonging survival despite incurable illness, at <u>some point</u> in the progression of an illness, this model of acute care is not the right model. The point at which the potential benefits of the acute care treatment model are outweighed by its burdens and/or lack of clear benefits is as individual as the person who lives with the illness. The best service model for healthcare would allow individualization of health services, particularly for persons who have advanced illness, so that each person gets the care that matters most to him or her. Unfortunately, in our current healthcare delivery model, patients seriously ill with a progressive illness are all too often presented with an either/or choice when it comes to planning for care. That is, either they stay in the current acute care model and get all that high-tech medicine can deliver or they give up the acute care model and focus exclusively on the goal of comfort. So, to actually improve care planning, not only do we need to make care planning part of the routine process of healthcare but also, for those individuals who have advanced illness, we need to be able to create a more flexible health delivery system so that each person can make individualized care plans that take advantage of all the medical treatment that might improve survival and function but effectively refuse those treatments that come with too much burden, too low a probability of benefit, or loss of dignity.

It is exactly this simultaneous change of providing planning conversations and the flexibility of options that has been created in La Crosse. In La Crosse, patients are provided the opportunity to create personal health plans about future medical care. Most, but not all, accept that opportunity at some point. The plans that are created are not about giving up treatment; rather, they are about tailoring treatment according to the values, goals, and illnesses of all people. Some patients have reasons to continue to push for all treatment. Others see diminishing returns for treatment and want to focus more on comfort and relationships. Still others may want to continue to try some treatments but forgo others. In each and every case, these are decisions people make with those they consider family. In this way, each family can focus on the support of this loved one and not get caught in arguments or anguish.

To put this in human terms, the typical story line in La Crosse is different from the one described at the beginning of this chapter. The story line in La Crosse is now that we know what the patient wants and we know what choices to make. This, of course, does not take away the sadness and grief of loss and death, but it does bring comfort in knowing that our decisions represented the values and goals of the person we loved and that our own actions were both respectful and loving.

Put simply, this is just better healthcare . . . healthcare that every American deserves to have. And unlike most other improvements in healthcare, the evidence suggests that this approach, in the overall picture, will reduce the waste that is making healthcare unaffordable for us all. This is the care model we should each want for our own families and for ourselves. This is one change in the healthcare system that we cannot afford to allow divisive politics to derail. If we do, we and our families will all suffer for it.

Bernard J. Hammes, PhD, received his BA and PhD in philosophy from the University of Notre Dame. Currently, he serves as the director of Medical Humanities and Respecting Choices at Gundersen Health System and Gundersen Lutheran Medical Foundation. He is currently the chair of the National POLST Paradigm Task Force and vice president of the International Society of Advance Care Planning and End of Life Care. He is also a professor of clinical science at the University of Wisconsin–La Crosse, an associate adjunct professor of the Institute for Health and Society at the Medical College of Wisconsin, and a clinical assistant professor in the Department of Pediatrics at the University of Wisconsin School of Medicine and Public Health.

References

1.   Physician Orders for Life-Sustaining Treatment paradigm. http://www.polst.org. Accessed May 13, 2009.

2.   Hickman SE, Nelson CA, Perrin NA, Moss AH, Hammes BJ, Tolle SW. A comparison of methods to communicate treatment preferences in nursing facilities: traditional practices versus the Physician Orders for Life-Sustaining Treatment program. *Journal of the American Geriatrics Society.* 2010;58(7):1241-1248.

3.   Hammes BJ, Rooney BL, Gundrum JD, Hickman SE, Harter N. The POLST program: a retrospective review of the demographics of use and outcomes in one community where advance directives are prevalent. *Journal of Palliative Medicine.* In press.

4. La Crosse Region Power of Attorney for Healthcare document [online]. http://www.gundluth.org/upload/docs/Services/POAHCVersionAEE81.pdf. Accessed September 6, 2011.

5. Hammes BJ, Briggs LA. *Building a systems approach to advance care planning.* La Crosse, WI: Gundersen Lutheran Medical Foundation; 2011.

6. Hammes BJ, Rooney BL, Gundrum JD. A comparative, retrospective, observational study of the prevalence, availability, and specificity of advance care plans in a county that implemented an advance care planning microsystem. *Journal of the American Geriatrics Society.* 2010;58(7):1249-1255.

7. Detering KM, Hancock AD, Reade MC, Silvester W. The impact of advance care planning on end of life care in elderly patients: randomised controlled trial. *BMJ.* 2010;340:c1345.

8. Wright AA, Zhang B, Ray A, et al. Associations between end-of-life discussions, patient mental health, medical care near death, and caregiver bereavement adjustment. *JAMA: Journal of the American Medical Association.* 2008;300(14):1665-1673.

9. Molloy DW, Guyatt GH, Russo R, et al. Systematic implementation of an advance directive program in nursing homes: a randomized controlled trial. *JAMA: Journal of the American Medical Association.* 2000;283(11):1437-1444.

three

Helping Individuals Make Informed Healthcare Decisions: The Role of the Advance Care Planning Facilitator

—Linda A. Briggs, MS, MA, RN

LIKE MOST AMERICANS, you probably know what a living will is. This type of advance directive (AD) allows you to provide instructions for life-sustaining treatment only when you are terminally ill or permanently unconscious. The other (and preferred) AD is a power of attorney for healthcare, which allows you to appoint a trusted individual (e.g., an agent or proxy) to make healthcare decisions for you if you become unable. Despite your awareness of your rights to complete a written plan, only 18% to 36% of you have participated in this activity.[1-3] Moreover, only one in three people living with serious advanced illness (and at risk of imminent complications) has created a plan regarding future treatment decisions.[4]

There are many reasons why you have not exercised your legal right to complete an AD.[5] You may feel that you can wait until you are older, or become sick, or get "sicker." You may believe that your loved ones know what kind of care you would want if you could not communicate and you feel no urgency to act any further. Some of you may want to talk about these issues with your family yet fear you will upset them. On a more emotional level, you may not know how, where, or when to bring up the subject of "dying."

On the other hand, some of you will say, "I've already done that," meaning you have completed an AD. You may have a sense of security that it is done, placed in a safe place (e.g., file cabinet or safe-deposit box) and out of sight. You hope never to have to use it. However, how confident are you that it will control the kind of care you receive in your last weeks, months, or years of life? Does it say what you want it to say? Are you comfortable your loved ones and healthcare providers will follow your decisions? What kind of conversations have you had with your loved ones about your personal goals and values?

Perhaps you are waiting for your doctor or other healthcare provider to talk to you about ADs. After all, if they were that important, surely your doctor would inform you and help get you started. There are many reasons why doctors and other healthcare providers do not initiate planning conversations. Many feel unskilled and uncomfortable initiating discussions.[6-9] Others may assume that patients are not interested in these types of discussions or fear that they will cause anxiety and stress.[10,11] Additionally, practical challenges such as insufficient time and reimbursement make it difficult for busy healthcare providers to focus on planning discussions in their daily work.[12,13]

In the 1980s, people living in La Crosse, Wisconsin, held similar concerns and beliefs about the value of ADs. The culture in this Midwestern community has changed dramatically since that time. In the early 1990s, the leaders of the La Crosse advance care planning (ACP) program decided to take a unique approach to the completion of ADs. They rejected the belief that this was a simple activity based only on an individual's legal right to complete a planning document. Instead, a robust and patient-centered planning process was designed that focused on quality discussions initiated by qualified healthcare professionals. A cornerstone of the program's success was the creation of a new healthcare role, the ACP facilitator. These individuals receive training in the necessary communication skills to assist individuals in making informed healthcare choices in light of personal goals, values, and beliefs. Working in partnership with physicians, trained facilitators make it possible to realistically deliver a consistent and reliable ACP service to individuals at all stages of illness and in a variety of outpatient and community settings. This ACP service has features that are distinctly different from typical AD programs.

Advance Care Planning versus Advance Directives: What's the Difference?

It is understandable if you are unaware of the differences between "advance care planning" and "advance directives." In fact, the literature sometimes uses these terms interchangeably. The distinction between them is critical and at the heart of wide variation in the quality of care planning services available to consumers. ACP and AD services vary in their goals, content, and outcomes.

Advance Directives: What Is Involved?

A typical AD service has the goal of helping people complete a written document that meets the state's legal requirements. Such standardized forms are often difficult to understand, written in "legalese," and provide little direction for how to make healthcare decisions. Individuals assisting with the completion of ADs are trained to ensure that such documents have the necessary signatures, dates, and other legal requirements. Healthcare organizations are motivated to comply with federal mandates and regulatory agencies. Therefore, when you are admitted as a patient to a hospital, you are asked whether you have an AD and, if so, where it can be found. If you have not completed an AD, you are asked whether you would like more information or assistance in this activity. Through this series of yes or no questions, organizations comply with federal regulations; however, the timing of these questions is not ideal. As a newly admitted patient, you are ill, uninterested, and unmotivated to participate in planning discussions. AD services may also be provided by an attorney as part of estate planning but disconnected from your doctors and medical care you receive. AD services often have a just-get-it-done attitude that gives individuals a false sense of security that what is "done" will be effective at a future point in time. Tools that have been developed to assist with the completion of ADs include brochures, videos, computer-based tutorials, educational presentations, and workshops. These single-modality interventions have not proved effective at helping individuals make informed healthcare decisions or, more importantly, ensuring that their decisions will be honored when needed.[14,15]

If you are among the minority of Americans who have completed a written AD, the research on the effectiveness of these documents may surprise you. The existence of a planning document does not ensure that you will receive the care you intend if you become seriously ill. For example, in a study of bereaved family members where 70% of patients had completed an AD, significant gaps in end-of-life care were found.[16] There are typically two reasons why written plans are not helpful: (1) chosen agents/proxies are unprepared to make healthcare decisions for another person, resorting to more aggressive care than the patient would choose, and (2) the written plan contains instructions that are too vague or ambiguous to guide clinical decision making.[17,18]

ADs don't work the way most people intend them to work. They fall short of providing the type of planning discussions that allow patient choice, comfort, and control in the last weeks, months, and years of life.

Advance Care Planning: What's Involved?

As the term "advance care planning" implies, it is a process and not an event. The La Crosse Respecting Choices ACP program has developed and tested a robust planning approach that involves patient-centered discussions and has broad and comprehensive goals:

- To provide qualified assistance to individuals in making informed healthcare choices appropriate to their stage of illness and their goals, values, and beliefs;
- To create plans that will be effective in providing personalized care—plans that ensure that individuals receive *all* the treatment and *only* the treatment they desire; and
- To develop strategies to communicate these choices to those who need to know (e.g., healthcare agent, family, physician, other healthcare providers).

To reach these goals, ACP requires communication. ACP is an interactive process of understanding, reflection, and discussion.

1. **Understanding.** While ADs focus on the completion of a planning document, ACP begins with the information individuals need to make personal healthcare decisions and motivate them to participate. Basically, individuals need to understand *why* ACP is important, *what* is involved, and *how* to begin the process. For healthy adults, the planning process is fairly straightforward; however, individuals living with advanced illness face complex and confusing choices. Treatments have benefits and burdens that must be understood and balanced against individuals' goals and values. Alternatives to treatments, including options for comfort care, must be explored. For example, if an individual chooses not to go back on a breathing machine for a lung complication, how will his or her symptoms be managed, and where will he or she be cared for? Contrary to the belief that patients are uninterested in receiving detailed information about the healthcare decisions they are asked to make, a recent survey showed that 75% of Americans are concerned about not having adequate information about treatment options.[19] Individuals desire and have the right to receive facts and medical advice on the critical decisions that will have a profound impact on their quality of life.[20]

2. **Reflection.** Healthcare decision making can be complex, especially for those with serious illness. Individuals need time to reflect on their personal goals, values, and beliefs as they relate to the information they are provided. For most individuals, quality of life is as important as length of life. How do you define quality of life? What activities and experiences give your life meaning? What goals are you hoping to achieve? What religious or cultural beliefs do you have? Individuals need adequate time to reflect on these important questions that will ultimately guide their personal decisions.

3. **Discussion.** Individuals also need time to discuss these issues with others who are important in the decision-making process, such as chosen healthcare agents/proxies, loved ones, doctors, and religious advisors. Without participating in ACP discussions, healthcare agents, for example, are typically unprepared to make critical life-and-death decisions for a loved one. The responsibility of making healthcare decisions can be overwhelming, causing stress and grief that can last for years.[21] Additionally, individuals with strong religious beliefs may want to talk with their minister, rabbi, or priest to receive guidance in making treatment decisions.

As an interactive process of understanding, reflection, and discussion, ACP resembles the familiar informed consent practices used to help patients understand recommended treatments or procedures, such as elective surgery, treatment for cancer, or management of heart failure. Could you imagine agreeing to a surgical procedure that you did not understand or not taking the time to talk to a surgeon about risks and complications? You have a right to the best medical facts available regarding your treatment choices. Armed with accurate information, you are more prepared to make your own choices and control your destiny. Consider the following example. Patients living with advanced illness are commonly asked whether they would want CPR if their heart or breathing stopped. This question is routinely asked on admission to a nursing home or hospital with the expectation that a yes or no answer will be given. Have you considered this question for yourself? What information would you need to make a decision about CPR? Would you want to know how successful it is at restarting the heart and breathing? Would you want to know the complications that can occur from CPR? Would you like the time to talk to your doctor about his or her recommendations? If you decided you did not want CPR, what alternative plans would need to be developed? How would you prepare your loved ones to follow your CPR decision? Decisions about life-sustaining treatments do not have simple yes or no answers.

This approach to ACP makes a difference for patients and families. Studies evaluating the impact of facilitated ACP discussions have demonstrated improved quality of life for patients, reduction in stress and anxiety for healthcare agents, and increased satisfaction with overall medical care.[22,23]

To achieve these outcomes, an ACP service requires skill, time, and organizational support. A core component of the success of the Respecting Choices ACP program is the creation of the role of the ACP facilitator, trained to assess individual planning needs, fears, goals, values, and beliefs and craft a patient-centered planning approach. The ACP facilitator provides this service as a member of the healthcare team, making referrals to others as needed and involving physicians whenever necessary.

The Team Approach to ACP and the Emerging Role of the ACP Facilitator

There is a tendency to assign the sole responsibility of ACP to the patient's physician. While this approach may have some advantages, significant barriers make this assignment unsustainable. In a small quality improvement study conducted at Gundersen Health System, several physicians were interviewed regarding their ACP practice for patients with advanced illness. Most physicians acknowledged the importance of initiating ACP discussions but admitted that they rarely had the time to do this consistently and focused on patients perceived to be at the highest risk for complications. Physicians who had access to nonphysician ACP facilitators were more likely to rely on this member of the team to make referrals. Even if physicians feel prepared, motivated, and willing to initiate ACP discussions, they will face challenges in delivering this service to *all* patients who need it as a result of increasing demands on physician-dependent services and lack of adequate reimbursement. This physician-based model of providing ACP is unsustainable and unreliable in delivering a consistent and reliable ACP service as a routine of care.

Respecting Choices advocates a different model—one that integrates a team approach to ACP and includes the physician but supports the training of nonphysicians in the role of ACP facilitator. A facilitator's role is to make it *easier* for you to make healthcare decisions, to *support* you in getting the information you need, to *help* you develop questions for your doctor, and to *guide* the creation of your personal healthcare plan. An ACP facilitator

- Initiates opportunities for ACP discussions at multiple encounters and throughout the life span of an individual;
- Assesses the needs of the individual seeking ACP assistance;
- Designs a patient-centered approach to planning based on the patient's illness, readiness to participate, fears and concerns, and religious or cultural beliefs;
- Makes referrals to other resources, as needed;
- Assists patients in making informed healthcare decisions based on facts, understanding, reflection, and discussion;
- Prepares the patient's healthcare agent and loved ones to understand and honor choices that the patient has made;
- Assists in the development of a plan that honors the patient's goals, values, and beliefs for future medical care; and
- Develops strategies to effectively communicate the plan to those who will be responsible for interpreting it and making decisions (e.g., healthcare agent, physician, and other healthcare providers).

The ACP facilitator cannot work alone. The delivery of quality healthcare services to patients is often complex, requiring a multidisciplinary team approach to achieve maximum outcomes. Using the expertise, background, and availability of a variety of qualified professionals, the patient is more likely to receive comprehensive and consistent care. There are many clinical examples of the effectiveness of this model. Consider the patient with chronic heart failure who suffers a heart attack. While the internist or hospitalist may initially diagnose the problem, cardiologists are consulted to assess the treatment options and make recommendations for a medical plan of care. The patient will be assisted by a rehabilitation team of nurses, physical therapists, and others who will design a plan for recovery and return to an active lifestyle. Additionally, a clinic heart failure team may be used to educate the patient in self-care, such as diet, exercise, and medication guidelines, as well as provide psychological and spiritual support.

Another common example is a patient newly diagnosed with diabetes. While the medical plan of care is designed by the patient's physician and a pharmacist consulted on the options for delivery of medications, the services of a diabetic educator are used for patient education and ongoing support in managing this chronic illness. This familiar team approach to quality patient care is effective for delivering a reliable ACP service, as well. The beneficiaries of this team approach to care are obviously the patient and his or her family, but professional satisfaction also increases as interdisciplinary respect and collaboration result in improved patient outcomes.

ACP facilitators work in a variety of community and healthcare settings. They are community volunteers, parish nurses, chaplains, social workers, and nurses. Their specific ACP duties will vary with their expertise and background and the planning needs of the individual.

Advance Care Planning Is Not
a One-Size-Fits-All Process

One of the greatest misconceptions about ACP is that it is a static process that ends with the completion of a written document—that it is a one-size-fits-all process. Many AD programs, tutorials, and documents propose a single planning approach for everyone. It is unrealistic and impossible to plan for all possibilities in a single document or at a single point in time. Respecting Choices defines ACP as a patient-centered process of understanding, reflection, and discussion. The content of this process will change over time as an individual moves from a healthy state to one of advanced illness. As goals and values change over the course of advanced illness, specific and timely planning strategies must be available.

To address the changing needs of patients for planning assistance over the course of their lives, Respecting Choices has developed a staged approach to ACP: First Steps, Next Steps, and Last Steps. This approach is based on an individual's stage of health, readiness to learn, and venue of care. This patient-centered and practical approach to planning makes it possible for individuals to take one step at a time, making decisions that are appropriate to their stage of illness and revising plans as necessary. This staged approach to planning also makes it possible to train ACP facilitators from varying backgrounds and expertise to assist individuals in making appropriate healthcare decisions in the community and healthcare setting.

First Steps Planning and
the Role of the ACP Facilitator

While any person over the age of 18 has the right to complete an AD, First Steps planning should be routinely initiated for those between the ages of 55 and 65 years as a component of routine healthcare. The goals of this stage of planning are to

- Introduce the importance of ACP as an ongoing process,
- Assist in the selection and preparation of a qualified agent/proxy,
- Explore the individual's goals for life-sustaining treatment in the event of a severe neurologic illness where a full cognitive recovery is unlikely, and
- Complete an AD (i.e., power of attorney for healthcare).

A First Steps ACP facilitator would assist you in several ways. You would be provided written information that helps you understand why planning is important; explore examples of situations that require healthcare decisions; reflect on personal goals, values, and religious beliefs; and identify fears or concerns you have about participating in such ACP discussions. The facilitator would help you choose a healthcare agent wisely—one who is willing to talk with you, who will follow your wishes, and who is capable of making decisions under stressful situations. An ACP meeting would be scheduled with you, your chosen healthcare agent(s), and other family members, as desired. The goal of this meeting would be to assist you in talking to your loved ones and to improve your agent's ability to make decisions consistent with your values and beliefs. The facilitator would also be attentive to possible obstacles to making advance care planning decisions. Perhaps you have family members who would disagree with your decisions or you have strong religious beliefs about withholding artificial nutrition and hydration. The facilitator would help create strategies to address these issues. In helping you create a written plan that reflects your goals, values, and beliefs, the facilitator will recommend strategies to communicate your personal plan to your healthcare agent, family, doctor, and other healthcare organizations.

First Steps facilitators may be in the community (e.g., senior center staff, parish nurses, volunteers), where they provide education on the importance of preplanning and the tools that are available to begin this work and complete a written AD, even when you are healthy. First Steps facilitators are also nurses, social workers, and chaplains who provide ACP services as a component of routine primary healthcare in the clinic setting.

First Steps ACP delivers an important message to patients: planning will be ongoing. It forces you to plan for advanced illness when you are healthy. It sets the foundation for weaving ACP discussions into the routines of care and helps to normalize the conversation.

Next Steps Planning and the Role of the ACP Facilitator

Many Americans suffer from advanced illness, such as heart failure, emphysema, or kidney disease. Due to advances in medical science and technology, such illnesses are well managed for years. Even so, since there are no cures for advanced illnesses, they will progress and eventually cause complications, a decline in people's ability to care for themselves, and repeated emergency department visits or hospitalizations. When these types of changes occur, it is time for a different planning approach—one that is specific to your illness and the real treatment decisions you will need to make when complications occur.

Consider the following example. John is a patient with emphysema, a type of advanced lung disease that makes him susceptible to pneumonia and breathing problems. His lung disease has been well managed until the past several months. His illness has worsened, and he has experienced repeated episodes of breathing complications that require hospitalizations and mechanical assistance to help his lungs recover. These episodes have taken a toll on his lungs, and he does not fully recover his ability to do the things he used to do. Life is not the same. As John's quality of life changes, he may begin to wonder, "Do I want to go back on a breathing machine again? Do I have other choices to help me breathe when I have a complication? How can my breathing symptoms be managed if I decide not to go back on the breathing machine again? How do I help my family understand my fears?" John needs assistance in navigating such challenges. Without assistance, John may be unaware of his choices and unable to make decisions. He will experience another medical crisis, and his family will be unprepared to make decisions on his behalf. He may or may not receive the care that he wants.

At this critical stage of John's illness, a Next Steps ACP facilitator will schedule a planning meeting with him, his chosen healthcare agent(s), and other family, if needed, in the outpatient setting when he is medically stable. The goals of this planning meeting are to help John understand his disease progression, potential complications, and life-sustaining treatments that may be needed if complications occur. His fears, hopes for living well, and experiences will be explored. While hoping for the best, John will be assisted in planning for worst-case scenarios and identifying the burdens that he is willing (or not willing) to accept. A critical component of Next Steps discussions is the preparation of the chosen healthcare agent to make future decisions consistent with John's goals, values, and beliefs and to make referrals to other resources that can help John live out the rest of his life with dignity. The planning process results in a disease-specific written plan that will be added to John's AD.

This Next Steps planning approach has resulted in improved understanding of treatment choices between patients and their chosen agents and a high level of satisfaction with the quality of such discussions.[24,25]

Last Steps Planning and the Role of the ACP Facilitator

As individuals age, become frail, and cope with multiple illnesses, they are at risk of complications that may result in death or disability. These individuals are often living in long-term care facilities and in danger of losing their ability to make their own healthcare decisions. Timing is of the essence. Last Steps facilitators assist individuals in clarifying goals of care and making specific decisions about CPR, hospitalization, management of breathing complications, and artificial nutrition and hydration, among other issues. Last Steps ACP facilitators are typically nurses, nurse practitioners, social workers, chaplains, and physicians who work in a variety of healthcare settings, such as long-term care facilities, home and hospice care, and palliative care. To ensure that patients' decisions are followed, the Physician Orders for Life-Sustaining Treatment (POLST) form (http://www.polst.org) is used to document specific treatment decisions in a system that converts them to medical orders that can be followed throughout the healthcare community.

ACP facilitators have unique roles to play at each stage of planning. By working in partnership with physicians and other healthcare providers, patients are provided the information, support, and freedom they need to choose the care that matches their goals and preserves their personal dignity. Physicians and healthcare providers know what treatment patients do and do not want. Care is individualized. Everyone benefits.

Advance Care Planning: A Worthy Investment?

Of course, not everyone will agree that the robust ACP service described herein is worth the investment. What is the motivation to support the role of the ACP facilitator? Why should an organization commit the necessary time for ACP? What is the return on investment? After all, reimbursement for ACP planning has met resistance over fears of so-called death panels and rationed healthcare. While these fears are unwarranted, they stem from a lack of consensus about the goals of an ACP service, which are to assist individuals to take control of their own healthcare and to make decisions based on facts and on their personal definitions of quality of life. When there is consensus about this personalized approach to planning, fears diminish, and a new paradigm for how to deliver this service emerges. ACP is understood as more than the completion of an advance directive. ACP discussions are patient centered. Patients' goals and values are revisited at appropriate points in time as they move from a healthy state to one of advanced illness. Written plans become more specific as advanced illness progresses, and they provide instructions to effectively guide clinical decision making. Loved ones are prepared to make decisions when serious illness occurs. The planning needs of individuals are met by multiple professionals and in different settings of care. A team approach that integrates the role of the ACP facilitator is efficient, practical, and rewarding for patients, families, and healthcare providers.

Life is precious. Only you can control the kind of care you receive in the last weeks, months, or years of your life. The ACP service described in this chapter creates a partnership with you, your doctor, qualified facilitators, and your loved ones to help you take charge of your life. ACP discussions promote trust and peace of mind, as depicted in the following message to a facilitator after an ACP discussion:

> *"I just wanted to thank you again for helping my dad. The meeting was just what we needed. It would have been difficult to broach those subjects without you there to facilitate. I think his mind was put at ease by getting everything out in the open, and it led to some very productive and loving conversations later in the day."*

This is the type of human interaction patients expect and deserve. Patient-centered ACP discussions have the power to heal and alleviate the stress and burdens of healthcare decision making.

Is ACP a worthy investment? You decide.

Linda Briggs is a master's-prepared nurse with 25 years of experience in critical care as a staff nurse, clinical nurse specialist, and educator. She received her MSN from the University of Wisconsin, Madison, and an MA in bioethics from the Medical College of Wisconsin in Milwaukee. Ms. Briggs joined the Respecting Choices team as the associate director in 1999. In this role, she is responsible for curriculum development and provides consultation and education to assist organization and community leaders interested in implementing the nationally recognized advance care planning program Respecting Choices. Her research has been focused on the disease-specific planning needs of patients with advanced illness and their families. Ms. Briggs has coauthored several Respecting Choices manuals and has published numerous articles related to end-of-life decision making.

References

1. Hawkins NA, Ditto PH, Danks JH, Smucker WD. Micromanaging death: process preferences, values, and goals in end-of-life medical decision making. *Gerontologist*. 2005;45(1):107-117.

2. Hickman SE, Hammes BJ, Moss AH, Tolle SW. Hope for the future: achieving the original intent of advance directives. *Hastings Center Report*. 2005;Spec No:S26-30.

3. Jennings B. Preface: improving end of life care: why has it been so difficult? *Hastings Center Report*. 2005;Spec No:S2-S4.

4. Bravo G, Dubois MF, Paquet M. Advance directives for health care and research: prevalence and correlates. *Alzheimer Disease and Associated Disorders*. 2003;17(4):215-222.

5. Schickedanz AD, Schillinger D, Landefeld CS, Knight SJ, Williams BA, Sudore RL. A clinical framework for improving the advance care planning process: start with patients' self-identified barriers. *Journal of the American Geriatrics Society*. 2009;57(1):31-39.

6. Csikai EL, Raymer M. Social workers' educational needs in end-of-life care. *Social Work in Health Care*. 2005;41(1):53-72.

7. Mohan D, Alexander SC, Garrigues SK, Arnold RM, Barnato AE. Communication practices in physician decision-making for an unstable critically ill patient with end-stage cancer. *Journal of Palliative Medicine*. 2010;13(8):949-956.

8. Thacker KS. Nurses' advocacy behaviors in end-of-life nursing care. *Nursing Ethics*. 2008;15(2):174-185.

9. Yedidia MJ. Transforming doctor-patient relationships to promote patient-centered care: lessons from palliative care. *Journal of Pain and Symptom Management*. 2007;33(1):40-57.

10. Curtis JR, Patrick DL, Caldwell ES, Collier AC. Why don't patients and physicians talk about end-of-life care? Barriers to communication for patients with acquired immunodeficiency syndrome and their primary care clinicians. *Archives of Internal Medicine.* 2000;160(11):1690-1696.

11. Hancock K, Clayton JM, Parker SM, et al. Discrepant perceptions about end-of-life communication: a systematic review. *Journal of Pain and Symptom Management.* 2007;34(2):190-200.

12. Legare F, Ratte S, Gravel K, Graham ID. Barriers and facilitators to implementing shared decision-making in clinical practice: update of a systematic review of health professionals' perceptions. *Patient Education and Counseling.* 2008;73(3):526-535.

13. Vieder JN, Krafchick MA, Kovach AC, Galluzzi KE. Physician-patient interaction: what do elders want? *Journal of the American Osteopathic Association.* 2002;102(2):73-78.

14. Lorenz K, Lynn J, Morton SC, et al. End-of-life care and outcomes. *Evidence Report/Technology Assessment (Summary).* 2004;(110)(110):1-6.

15. Wenger NS, Shugarman LR, Wilkinson A. Advance directives and advance care planning: report to Congress, August 2008. http://aspe.hhs.gov/daltcp/reports/2008/adcongrpt.htm. Accessed August 24, 2011.

16. Teno JM, Gruneir A, Schwartz Z, Nanda A, Wetle T. Association between advance directives and quality of end-of-life care: a national study. *Journal of the American Geriatrics Society.* 2007;55(2):189-194.

17. Fagerlin A, Schneider CE. Enough. The failure of the living will. *Hastings Center Report.* 2004;34(2):30-42.

18. Shalowitz DI, Garrett-Mayer E, Wendler D. The accuracy of surrogate decision makers: a systematic review. *Archives of Internal Medicine.* 2006;166(5):493-497.

19. *National Journal.* Living well at the end of life: a national conversation, 2011. http://syndication.national journal.com/communications/NationalJournalRegenceToplines.pdf. Accessed August 26, 2011.

20. Pfeifer MP, Mitchell CK, Chamberlain L. The value of disease severity in predicting patient readiness to address end-of-life issues. *Archives of Internal Medicine.* 2003;163(5):609-612.

21. Wendler D, Rid A. Systematic review: the effect on surrogates of making treatment decisions for others. *Annals of Internal Medicine.* 2011;154(5):336-346.

22. Detering KM, Hancock AD, Reade MC, Silvester W. The impact of advance care planning on end of life care in elderly patients: randomised controlled trial. *BMJ*. 2010;340:c1345.

23. Wright AA, Zhang B, Ray A, et al. Associations between end-of-life discussions, patient mental health, medical care near death, and caregiver bereavement adjustment. *JAMA: Journal of the American Medical Association*. 2008;300(14):1665-1673.

24. Kirchhoff KT, Hammes BJ, Kehl KA, Briggs LA, Brown RL. Effect of a disease-specific planning intervention on surrogate understanding of patient goals for future medical treatment. *Journal of the American Geriatrics Society*. 2010;58(7):1233-1240.

25. Lyon ME, Garvie PA, Briggs L, He J, McCarter R, D'Angelo LJ. Development, feasibility, and acceptability of the family/adolescent-centered (FACE) advance care planning intervention for adolescents with HIV. *Journal of Palliative Medicine*. 2009;12(4):363-372.

four

Honoring Choices Minnesota: A Metropolitan Program Underway

—Kent S. Wilson, MD, and Sue A. Schettle

MAKING COMPLEX MEDICAL decisions at a time of crisis is stressful for the patient, for family members, and for the team providing the healthcare. When patients cannot speak for themselves, the level of stress increases, especially when family members do not know what the patient would have wanted. Advance care planning is a process that provides the opportunity for patients to have conversations with family members or other loved ones about their healthcare choices if they were not able to speak for themselves. It's a process that can empower patients, families, and loved ones and lead to more informed care decisions for patients.

Gundersen Health System, a physician-led, not-for-profit healthcare system based in La Crosse, Wisconsin, chose to improve this advance care planning process on a systems level. The result was its Respecting Choices model of care. Careful review of Gundersen Health System's model demonstrates the indisputable merits of the approach: the model has achieved exceptional, documented success in patient discussions and planning with the help of a trained facilitator, tracking patients' preferences in their medical records, and ultimately helping providers to honor patients' wishes.

The comparison of Gundersen Health System's results with national averages underscores the need for application of like models throughout the nation. Despite the clear success of Respecting Choices in La Crosse, the question of scalability remained: could the model be successfully adapted and implemented in a large metropolitan area?

The Twin Cities Medical Society took on that challenge by launching a collaborative, comprehensive, multiyear effort to bring the successes of the Gundersen Health System model to a diverse and heavily populated metropolitan area. The resulting program aims to ensure that all adults in the community have access to advance care planning and that infrastructure supports efforts to ensure that advance directives are followed by healthcare professionals.

This chapter describes how the Twin Cities model, Honoring Choices Minnesota (HCM), came into being. It reviews the medical society's decision to sponsor this effort, how broader support for the project was created, training efforts, partnerships, and community engagement. The final section shares preliminary results from the first pilot year and looks ahead to what the future holds for this program.

We cannot yet know to what degree HCM can achieve the outcomes that were experienced in La Crosse. This will take many years. We can say, however, that, to date, an advance care planning program modeled on Respecting Choices is indeed scalable, and we expect that care will improve for patients in Minnesota.

Sponsorship: The Twin Cities Medical Society

The Twin Cities Medical Society (TCMS) represents 5,500 physicians living and/or practicing in the seven-county area that encompasses the twin cities of

Minneapolis and Saint Paul, Minnesota. This metro area has more than 2.7 million residents, more than a quarter of whom are over 55 years old; thus, the region offered an opportunity to implement Gundersen's approach on a significantly larger scale.[1]

A member-driven and grassroots-focused organization, the TCMS was formed in 2010 as a merger between the East Metro Medical Society and the West Metro Medical Society. The East Metro Medical Society Foundation has retained its name and, through the TCMS, serves as the convener and coordinator of HCM.

The mission of the TCMS is to connect, represent, and engage physicians in improving clinical practice, policy development, and public health initiatives.[2] Given these objectives, it was no surprise that the Respecting Choices model at Gundersen Health System struck a chord with the TCMS. After careful consideration of the initiatives, strategies, and outcomes of the Respecting Choices model, the TCMS took on the challenge of applying the approach in a new setting.

Honoring Choices Minnesota: The Synopsis

HCM is a collaborative, community-wide public health initiative led by the TCMS. It is a multiyear effort to inspire and support family conversations regarding end-of-life care planning and was first piloted at seven sites in 2010.

Its mission: to promote the benefits of advance care planning to the community at large and simultaneously implement processes and methods to support advance care planning.

The Idea Germinates

Inspired by the success of the Respecting Choices model, the idea for a similar advance care planning initiative in Minnesota had been left on the table by Dr. Robert Moravec, previous board president of the East Metro Medical Society Foundation. He recommended examining the Respecting Choices program at

La Crosse because HealthEast Care System, his employer, had experimented with a program inspired by Respecting Choices.

The TCMS knew that Allina Hospitals and Clinics and Park Nicollet Health Services had initiated pilot programs modeled after the Respecting Choices program. The idea was further bolstered by the 2008 Advance Directives and Advance Care Planning: Report to Congress,[3] which outlined problem areas and potential for improvement and mentioned positive results from Respecting Choices.

In February of 2008, board members of the East Metro Medical Society Foundation held a conference call with Dr. Bernard "Bud" Hammes, director of the Respecting Choices program, to learn more about the work being done at Gundersen. TCMS leaders carried out a site visit as part of a due-diligence examination. The TCMS reviewed the collaborative programs at both Gundersen and Mayo Clinic Health System: Franciscan Healthcare in La Crosse, Wisconsin. The lessons learned—collaboration, medical infrastructure development initially with embedded quality improvement mechanisms, followed by a later-stage public engagement program—were noted. Gundersen's results were compelling: the Respecting Choices program was able to document very high percentages of dying patients with advance care directives—directives that were followed a very high percentage of the time. Those results were reported in the *Journal of the American Geriatrics Society*.[4]

Subsequently, a randomized controlled trial of advance care planning modeled on the Respecting Choices approach has demonstrated major benefits with improved end-of-life care; patient and family satisfaction; and reduced stress, anxiety, and depression in surviving relatives.[5] More recently, Minnesota advance care planning and end-of-life issues have been discussed in an article by Howard Bell in *Minnesota Medicine,* the state medical association's journal.[6]

The TCMS was deeply inspired by the Respecting Choices model, but its board also had to acknowledge the fundamental differences between Gundersen's initial effort and a program that could thrive in a heavily populated, diverse metropolitan area. With this in mind, HCM incorporates (a) Respecting Choices concepts and methodologies, training systems, and materials, established through a formal contract with Gundersen, and (b) Minnesota-based healthcare directive, governance, and implementation.

Creating Honoring Choices Minnesota

On the basis of lessons learned from Gundersen's work in the La Crosse community, which included the need for a common healthcare directive and patient education materials, the TCMS's upscaled initiative was founded on the idea that a community approach to advance care planning necessitated three macrolevel steps:

1. **Infrastructure.** Develop and install systems in the healthcare community to encourage patient-centered planning processes that would generate conversations and develop advanced directives and then recognize those directives within the provider community.
2. **Training.** Healthcare professionals need to be trained to (a) encourage and facilitate the creation of advance directives, (b) verify the existence of advance directives for patients facing care decisions, and (c) adhere to those directives whenever possible.
3. **Engagement.** Once the infrastructure is in place and training is underway, the community must be engaged. This means facilitating both understanding of and comfort with the initiative.

Macrostep One: Building the Healthcare System Infrastructure

One aspect critical to the success so far has been the input of local experts who are already leading advance care planning programs within their respective organizations based on the Respecting Choices model. Both Allina Hospitals and Clinics and Park Nicollet Health Services began implementing the programs based on the Gundersen model prior to the launch of HCM. Both entities are combining the concepts and principles of the Gundersen model with the healthcare directive and other elements of HCM. The leadership, guidance, and commitment of both Allina and Park Nicollet have been invaluable in this initiative.

Building awareness and consensus

In July of 2008, HCM brought together 40 members of the Twin Cities healthcare community at the University of Minnesota's Saint Paul campus. The goal: to create awareness of the Gundersen model and gauge the interest level in collaborating and coordinating resources related to advance care planning. Attendees wholeheartedly and unanimously agreed that there was a need for this type of approach in the Twin Cities.

Building on this initial positive reaction, HCM organized a presentation for CEOs and other senior-level leaders from nearly every metro-area hospital system and health plan in September 2008. The presentation explained Gundersen's model and its outcomes and gave leaders a chance to ask questions.

On the basis of lessons learned from Gundersen Health System, TCMS leaders understood that a successful initiative had to be collaborative, not competitive. During the discussion, Brock Nelson, president and CEO of Regions Hospital, said, "We can't do this alone. If someone is willing to coordinate an advance care planning initiative for the community, we are willing to participate." Others were in agreement, and, by the end of the meeting, all present had unanimously committed to

- Not compete on advance care planning,
- Collaborate in the development of a community approach by using shared materials and processes, and
- Devote resources to the effort.

Advisory committee begins, guideline goals set

The enthusiasm of the provider community contributed to the momentum of the project, and a broadly representative advisory committee was formed in the fall of 2008. The committee included representatives from healthcare systems, insurers, nonprofit organizations, and community-based organizations. In May 2009, Honoring Choices Minnesota (HCM) was chosen as the name for the project and registered with the State of Minnesota. Over the next three months, several steps were taken: a logo was selected, patient education materials were ordered from Gundersen Health System, and a schedule of educational events was set. The advisory committee agreed to a conceptual work plan and developed a community standard for a new healthcare directive document that was standardized, compliant with Minnesota state law, clinically useful, and easy to read. The document was made available online for free in both English and Spanish.

During this time, the project also began to receive initial funding from healthcare organizations.

The Institute for Clinical Systems Improvement (ICSI) served as a key member of the advisory committee, as it was also starting work on revising palliative care guidelines. The ICSI is "an independent organization dedicated to transforming the healthcare system so it delivers patient-centered and value-driven care."[7] It set a goal of creating a model where palliative care is integrated into routine care for both primary care and specialty care and formed several pilots, one of which was designed to focus on advance care planning. The institute worked to coordinate its efforts with HCM.

Shared vision and objectives

While the implementation of HCM was separated from the forming years of Gundersen Health System's effort by demographics, geography, and two decades, they both set out with a common vision to improve care for patients and to focus efforts on patient-centered care plans.

Recruitment of pilot sites

HCM employed a recruitment program initially involving larger healthcare systems, including HealthPartners, Fairview, HealthEast, and Hennepin County Medical Center, each of which installed pilot programs. The six-month pilot provided experience to take the program systemwide.

The organizations decided which patient population(s) to use for piloting the program and identified individuals to be trained as facilitators and instructors. Workflows were defined and discussions occurred regarding the process of referrals to advance care planning facilitators and which quality measures to collect. These components were critical to the success of the pilot sites and served an important role in assuring system readiness.

Each pilot site's implementation plan was strategically tailored to meet the unique needs of its own community. While there are nuances in the sites' execution strategies and quantifiable objectives, the program dictates shared overarching vision and processes:

- Standardize the advance care planning process in a way that encourages clear communication.
- Identify a patient group for which a facilitated advance care planning discussion would be appropriate.
- Complete advance care planning discussions with the identified patients and their families.
- Increase the number of patients who have completed an advance care directive form (most sites seek to increase this number by as much as 50% over baseline).
- Track two quality measures (shared by all pilot programs): (1) the percentage of patients who had an advance care directive at the time of death and (2) the percentage of time the advance care directive document was found in the medical record when needed.
- Track time and costs to aid future discussions on reimbursement.

- Increase the transfer of patients' preferences (as expressed in directives) to appropriate medical orders.
- Seek feedback on the program via surveys or a rating system.

Macrostep Two: Training Pilot Site Participants

Pilot site teams attended institutional readiness trainings in summer and fall 2009 and facilitator and instructor training in fall 2009. Implementation plans were developed for each site with review and guidance from Respecting Choices faculty.

The following health plans participated in the HCM Advisory Committee:

- Blue Cross and Blue Shield of Minnesota
- HealthPartners
- UCare

Forty-six facilitators were trained and certified in late 2009 at the comprehensive training program. A facilitator's role is to initiate the advance care planning discussions with patients and their families. Ten individuals received additional training and were certified as instructors. An instructor not only can facilitate these discussions but also serves as an in-house expert who can train new facilitators. This is an important component to the overall sustainability of the community-wide effort.

As part of the HCM initiative, members of the healthcare community have been challenged to honor the following promises:

1. We will initiate the conversation.
2. We will provide assistance with advance care planning.
3. We will make sure plans are clear.
4. We will maintain and retrieve plans.
5. We will appropriately follow plans.

HCM licensed education materials from Gundersen's Respecting Choices program. Given the need to accommodate Minnesota governance and policy, local healthcare institutions and patient educators modified materials as appropriate. These materials are now available in five languages.

Macrostep Three: Community Engagement

The efforts of HCM have benefited significantly from two partnerships outside the healthcare community. Through collaboration with Twin Cities Public Television and the Citizens League, HCM has been able to disperse its core messages to a broader audience. The emphasis of the community engagement strategy is:

- **To Demystify** . . . taboo issues related to the death and dying processes in the twenty-first century,
- **To Inspire** . . . Minnesotans to imagine becoming more involved in the end-of-life care decision-making process,
- **To Model** . . . ways in which families can discuss and embrace end-of-life care planning,
- **To Support** . . . families with an online "tool kit" of video and text tools, and
- **To Prepare** . . . caregivers and families alike to make certain that family choices are always honored.

This partnership formed the core of a three-year public engagement campaign. Components of this multifaceted campaign include utilizing media, creating short documentaries and materials, getting feedback from individuals and segments of the community, and holding events.

Campaign features

- *Message spots*

  The campaign includes development of 30-second message spots featuring known and trusted Minnesotans discussing the advance care planning conversations they've had within their own families.

- *Content pods*

  Plans also include content pods, each featuring a 30-minute documentary accompanied by relevant online content as well as a complementary discussion on *Almanac*, Twin Cities Public Television's award-winning weekly public affairs show.

- *Listening sessions*

  The collaboration between Twin Cities Public Television, the Citizens League, and HCM has also produced a series of "Listening Sessions." Starting in August of 2010, these sessions engaged community members in discussions on the topic of end-of-life preferences. The goal: to remove some of the fear and awkwardness surrounding conversations on this topic.

As organizers found, although the issue of end-of-life preferences presents itself as a medical issue, choices are a complex product of social, emotional, spiritual, and cultural dynamics.

Four individual interviews were conducted, as well as discussions with seven groups of five to eight participants each. Participants were invited to the discussion groups because of their experiences with the dying process. As such, their views are not likely to be representative of the general public. However, the richness of their experiences suggests that their insights can provide meaningful guidance as the Honoring Choices project progresses. Several common themes emerged from their responses; together, these themes can be considered as potential key influencers on end-of-life preferences:

- There is a cultural bias against "giving up" that stymies family discussion and predisposes family decision makers (more so than the patient) to aggressive treatments.
- Advances in modern medicine are simultaneously giving rise to the urge to fight death and to understand and accept it.
- The significance of end-of-life decisions and the lack of experience in making them can create such overwhelming circumstances that people sometimes shy away from conversations for fear of saying the wrong thing.
- The instinct to protect one's family is very strong and may be one of the strongest influences on end-of-life preferences.
- Family dynamics have a powerful influence over medical choices. An individual's clearly expressed wishes can ease family stress and enable a more peaceful death.
- Discussing death or experiencing it in positive ways can reduce the fear of death and lead to more advanced decision making.
- Faith plays a vital role in guiding the dying process but less so in terms of medical choices.
- Interdisciplinary teams seem to be especially effective at easing families and their loved ones through the dying process.

Expanding leadership to engage the community

In February 2011, HCM received support in the form of a dedicated community engagement director. The individual in this role serves as the primary staff person and organizer for the project, with responsibilities ranging from budget management to community outreach.

Results to Date and Looking Ahead

Program effectiveness: early positive results

After the initial round of pilot sites in early 2010, the HCM team was tasked with researching and evaluating the effectiveness of the program. In July 2010, a conference was held in Minneapolis to present the outcomes and lessons learned of the HCM pilot teams.

Across the seven sites of the 2010 six-month pilot session, 607 patients were approached regarding advance care planning. Two hundred seven patients participated in facilitated discussions, and 102 patients completed advance care directives.

While each pilot site shared unique experiences, several nonquantifiable yet positive outcomes emerged.

Positive outcomes sampling

- Working relationships and stronger communications were developed across the Twin Cities healthcare community.
- Facilitators are comfortable with having dialogue with patients and families.
- Key departments were trained and aware of the initiative.
- The ability was demonstrated to modify infrastructure relatively quickly to develop a process that worked.
- Medical staff was very open to facilitations occurring.
- Patients who completed the facilitated advance care planning process were satisfied with the service.
- The budget allowed for training and supplies.
- Communication with all staff was important and prioritized.
- Pilot team members were enthusiastic.
- HCM added a valuable service to offer clinic patients.
- A standard place was created for documenting existence of healthcare directives.[8]

Another way of measuring success is the sheer volume of trained facilitators: fewer than three years after the initial phone call with Respecting Choices Director Bud Hammes, 500 healthcare professionals throughout the Twin Cities have already been trained to facilitate advance care directive conversations with patients and their families.[6]

Looking ahead, in 2011 a physician research director was appointed and research program developed. A second round of pilots was completed in the first half of 2011, so all hospitals and healthcare systems in the metro area have completed at least one pilot project.

Adapting Our Approach Based on What We Have Learned

HCM is constantly evolving due to feedback from pilot sites and members of the community. The 2011 pilot site program was adapted on the basis of lessons learned from the 2010 program, and revisions will continue to be made as the message reaches more of the community.

Broadening Community Engagement Strategies

A significant part of scaling to a diverse metropolitan area is understanding and then attending to the needs of the community. A strong focus of HCM: its engagement of groups who often fall outside of the traditional healthcare system, including various ethnic and religious communities. Going forward, HCM also aims to broaden community engagement strategies to reach those for whom the message may not be easily accessible, including many immigrant and refugee groups who now live in Minnesota. Fourteen more Listening Sessions were held in 2011 with various ethnic, religious, and multicultural communities throughout Minnesota. The goal is to understand the opportunities, as well as the barriers and drawbacks, for communities to engage in discussions about advance care planning. The content of these Listening Sessions is available on an interactive Web site (http://www.honoringchoices.org) that also contains tools and resources for community members. There is also a partnership with local media members to help broaden the message of HCM through public service announcements, as well as local newspaper coverage.

A dinner event held in September 2010 brought several new community members together with the healthcare community. Attendees included ethnic and religious representatives, lawyers, social services organizations, senior services groups, foundations, and other local organizations.

The medical society's hope is for the Twin Cities metro area, and eventually the state, to understand the importance of advance care planning and decision making and be familiar with HCM as a resource. Visit http://www.metrodoctors. com to find more information about the TCMS HCM program.

Kent Wilson, MD, is a retired otolaryngologist who practiced at Midwest Ear, Nose and Throat Specialists for more than 30 years. He served as the president of the Minnesota Academy of Otolaryngology, Head and Neck Surgery and as both trustee and president for the Minnesota Medical Association. He is currently the president of the East Metro Medical Foundation Board and the medical director of Honoring Choices Minnesota. Over the past three years, in his role with Honoring Choices, he has spent considerable time and effort growing the initiative, working with partners, and leading the advisory committee.

Sue A. Schettle is the first chief executive officer of the Twin Cities Medical Society, a physician membership organization representing more than 5,000 physicians from the seven-county metro area of St. Paul/Minneapolis. She also serves as the executive director of the East Metro Medical Foundation, West Metro Medical Foundation, and Minnesota Physician Services Inc. and as the project director for Honoring Choices Minnesota, a comprehensive community collaboration that works to promote advance care planning to Minnesotans.

References

1.   United States Census Bureau. 2006–2008 American Community Survey, Minneapolis–St. Paul–Bloomington, MN-WI metropolitan statistical area. http://factfinder.census.gov/servlet/ADPTable?_bm=y&-geo_id=31000US33460&-qr_name=ACS_2008_3YR_G00_DP3YR5&-context=adp&-ds_name=&-tree_id=3308&-_lang=en&-redoLog=false&-format=. Accessed August 29, 2011.

2.   Twin City Medical Society Web site. http://www.metrodoctors.com. Accessed August 29, 2011.

3.   Wenger NS, Shugarman LR, Wilkinson A. Advance directives and advance care planning: report to Congress, August 2008. http://aspe.hhs.gov/daltcp/reports/2008/adcongrpt.htm. Accessed August 24, 2011.

4.   Hammes BJ, Rooney BL, Gundrum JD. A comparative, retrospective, observational study of the prevalence, availability, and specificity of advance care plans in a county that implemented an advance care planning microsystem. *Journal of the American Geriatrics Society*. 2010;58(7):1249-1255.

5.   Detering KM, Hancock AD, Reade MC, Silvester W. The impact of advance care planning on end of life care in elderly patients: randomised controlled trial. *BMJ*. 2010;340:c1345.

6.   Bell H. Personalized medicine: without guidance from patients, medicine sustains life at any cost. *Minnesota Medicine*. 2011:22-27.

7.   Institute for Clinical Systems Improvement Web site. http://www.icsi.org. Accessed August 29, 2011.

8.   2010 Honoring Choices Minnesota pilot program summary. http://www.metrodoctors.com. Accessed August 29, 2011.

five

Respecting Patient Choices: Scaling Care Planning to a Whole Country

—William Silvester, MD

IN 2001, WHEN working as an intensive care specialist, I was struck by the care provided to three particular patients in the hospital. The first was an elderly man with advanced cancer who was admitted urgently to my intensive care unit (ICU) with severe pneumonia and ended up dying several days later while still on a mechanical ventilator. The man's family was very upset about how he suffered and said that he would never have wanted to die this way if someone had only bothered to ask him or the family.

The second case was an elderly woman with very advanced dementia who was transferred to the hospital with a fractured hip. She lay in a hospital bed in a fetal position for six weeks while the surgeons and anaesthetists were deciding whether she was fit for an operation to fix the fracture. She screamed in pain every time the nurses moved her for hygiene and skin protection. Eventually, the family members were the ones who begged the doctors to palliate, saying that this was not what she would have wanted.

A man in his mid-70s was admitted to a cancer ward one afternoon for chemotherapy for a recurrent cancer. He told the admitting doctor that he did not want cardiopulmonary resuscitation if he had a cardiac arrest. The doctor agreed to this but did not fill out a do-not-resuscitate form and did not tell the nursing staff. As I'm sure you could predict, he had a cardiac arrest in the early hours of the next morning and received 30 minutes of cardiac massage and other invasive procedures before the resuscitation was abandoned.

In all three cases the patients' wishes either were not known or were known and not respected, and, in all cases, the families were very upset about their family members' final hours or days. This triggered me to look for a solution to this perennial problem. Clearly, the solution lay in talking to patients about what they would want in the future before it was too late to ask them. When I began to comb through the literature, I discovered the concept of advance care planning. It was obvious that many attempts to deal with this problem were failing, but, within this sea of failure, I found a successful model: Respecting Choices from La Crosse, Wisconsin, led by Dr. Bud Hammes, the director of medical humanities, and Linda Briggs, an ethics consultant, at Gundersen Health System.

What particularly impressed me was the no-nonsense approach that these two took to ensuring that advance care planning was actually delivered. For example, they trained nonphysicians because they recognized that physicians have neither the time nor the inclination required to talk to their patients properly about what they might want in the future.

I telephoned Dr. Hammes and, after a number of conversations, invited him to come to Australia to teach us his unique approach.

After forming a steering committee, I succeeded in securing funds to bring Dr. Hammes and Ms. Briggs and their training program to my hospital for one week. The next six months were a hectic period of preparation. We formed a reference group; gained executive support; prepared policy and advance care planning documents; worked with key stakeholders within hospitals, such as the medical records department, on how these new documents would be filed; and, most importantly, gained the interest and support of the doctors and nurses in the clinical areas where the advance care planning model was to be trialled. The training date was set for August 2002.

I already recognized at this early stage that in order for this program to be funded into the future, it was essential to have political support. I was fortunate to be able to convince the Australian Government Federal Minister for Ageing, the honourable Kevin Andrews, to officially launch the program in August. His presence achieved three outcomes. First, it enabled me to obtain national television coverage of the launch through an Australian Broadcasting Corporation high-profile national current affairs program called *7:30 Report*. Second, it secured the political support required to get the Australian Government Federal Department of Health and Ageing to fund an expanded implementation. Third, it ensured that there would be no public perception that our advance care planning program was linked in any way to euthanasia. This was crucial because no federal or state government in Australia, then or now, would fund or want to be seen as linked to a program associated with euthanasia, which is illegal in Australia. Kevin Andrews was already known publicly as very opposed to euthanasia and would not risk being associated with a program that was pro-euthanasia.

Our program had already attracted the attention of the Australian Department of Health and Ageing in early 2002. During 2002 and early 2003, through negotiation and the demonstrated success of the one-year trial, the department agreed to fund approximately $1 million over the next three years to deliver three outcomes. They were (1) the implementation of advance care planning into a select number of aged care homes, (2) the trialling of advance care planning in community palliative care services, and (3) the implementation of advance care planning into one health service in each Australian state and territory (New South Wales, Queensland, South Australia, Western Australia, Tasmania, Northern Territory, and Australian Capital Territory).

In essence, what the federal government health department staff wanted me to do was to build the evidence that advance care planning was successful and, specifically, to demonstrate that this "American" model of advance care planning could work in Australia. The section of the department providing this funding was the branch responsible for provision of palliative care throughout Australia, and it saw the clear connection between advance care planning and good end-of-life care.

In order to expand Respecting Choices within Australian healthcare, I undertook two responsibilities. The first was to "Australianise" the program—adapt it to the conditions of the Australian healthcare system and the Australian psyche and language. We decided to call our model "Respecting Patient Choices" to differentiate it from the Gundersen program name and to ensure that there was no possible ambiguity in the public's mind about whose choices we were respecting. We also rewrote the training materials to reflect the relevant Australian health law and Australian legal and medical terminology.

The second responsibility was to secure the right to be able to use the intellectual property of the Respecting Choices program. Gundersen Lutheran Medical Foundation kindly agreed to license us to implement the program into multiple health services in Australia. From late 2003 to 2006, we delivered the program to multiple health services and aged care homes around Australia. This gave us the opportunity to progressively refine our materials and training workshops and also provided us valuable experience in how to prepare other healthcare organizations for the culture change required to effectively introduce advance care planning.

We recognized early on the importance of Respecting Patient Choices being seen as a national model. Therefore, we established the National Reference Group, with membership that consisted of important stakeholders and representatives from national peak bodies. This included the Australian Medical Foundation, the Australian Nursing Federation, learned colleges, bodies representing the palliative care and aged care sectors, and so on.

The second strategy to ensure a national focus was the formation of a national selection committee to choose those health services around the country in which the program was implemented. Again, this committee comprised representatives of peak bodies and learned colleges, as well as representatives of the federal government and of each state government into whose jurisdiction the program was being delivered. This ensured buy-in from the current program funder (the federal government) and from the future funders (each state government).

As the program was delivered to each selected state-based health service, we organized publicity through the media and made contact with relevant local politicians. The purpose of these strategies was twofold. It more rapidly built public and health professional awareness of advance care planning generally and Respecting Patient Choices specifically, and it helped to secure future funding support in each state. The media engagement was achieved by setting up an official launch of the new program at the health service, with the inauguration attended by newspaper, radio, and, if possible, television journalists. News stories ran in local media, and we made appearances, along with the identified local clinical champion, on local talkback radio. The ideal situation was to have the local politician and/or a senior local health department official conduct the official launch because this improved the media interest and accentuated the local buy-in. The meetings that I held with the state health ministers also increased the state health department interest in the program. The federal Department of Health and Ageing regarded its role in financing the implementation of the program at a pilot site in each state for one year as seed funding for a program that would then be sustained by ongoing funding from each state health department. This was made more likely if the state health minister or local politician, local media, and public interest (demonstrated through talkback radio) were supportive.

Throughout the national implementation of the state-based programs, I continued to engage, whenever possible, with the federal politicians and the Department of Health and Ageing. This was done by providing regular reports to the department officials and by either meeting with the federal ministers for health or ageing or asking them to participate in the official launches.

The other key element to strengthening political support was to explore any opportunity to gain media support for Respecting Patient Choices. Over the years, this has occurred through national radio and television programs and through newspapers with large circulations. The best hook to engaging the journalists was by providing great personal stories delivered by patients or the families of deceased patients whose wishes were known and respected at the end of life. I have invariably found that every person whom I have spoken to about advance care planning, including journalists and politicians, has identified with the inherent benefits through his or her own experience of the death of a family member or friend. The human connection always works.

Engaging with the media takes considerable time and effort and has been made much easier in recent times by employing a Respecting Patient Choices national communications director. This person, as a former prominent journalist, has the understanding of and the connections with the media world and is able to "work up" the stories and present them to the journalists. This has led to some great successes.

Over time, we have found that the key to the growth of advance care planning throughout Australia has been to encourage local ownership and self-propagation. Based on a train-the-trainer model, the system is intended to be self-sustaining; that is, once established in each health service, not only can it maintain its own program but also it is encouraged to expand it within its state to other health services and into aged care homes. We have always provided support to adapt advance care planning documentation, training materials, and policies to state legislation and local requirements. Not infrequently, as a consequence of local ownership and local funding requirements, programs have adopted their own names rather than using the Respecting Patient Choices name, a move we endorse if it ensures greater support and take up of advance care planning.

What have been the obstacles to the program along the way? The two greatest threats have been religious opposition and adequacy of funding. In 2005, when advance care planning was being trialled in aged care homes, questions were raised through the print media about whether Respecting Patient Choices was really a government-sponsored program to "pull the plug" on elderly aged care residents with dementia. Simultaneously, the same religious concerns were being raised with an influential federal senator who asked questions about the program in a federal parliamentary committee. These unwelcome aspersions caused dismay for the federal Department of Health and Ageing staff who were funding our program. Fortunately, I was able to demonstrate that the principles and policies that underwrote our program were aligned with the Australian Catholic Code of Ethics. I arranged to meet with the Australian Catholic Church bishops committee responsible for overseeing such things. Fortunately, over several meetings I was able to demonstrate that we were on common ground, and, indeed, the work that we were doing catalysed their committee to establish similar advance care planning documentation. Ultimately, we were thanked for our collaboration and support for their endeavours.

We had also established a national ethico-legal subcommittee of the Respecting Patient Choices National Reference Group. This committee, composed of several lawyers, ethicists, and members of the Respecting Patient Choices staff, was charged with overseeing the legal requirements, the documentation, and the ethical principles of the program as they were being implemented in each state. When questions were raised about the religious issues, we invited a nationally prominent Catholic ethicist to join the committee to identify and resolve any differences. This strategy assisted in demonstrating the common ground between us.

I think that funding will always be a struggle until the health professionals, health bureaucrats, and politicians see advance care planning as part of core business in healthcare. Despite our significant progress, many of the above are still not really aware of advance care planning, nor do they understand it. We still have senior decision makers who want to reduce funding either because they see it as an easy target or because they argue that the program is established and not in need of further funding, not realizing that penetration into core business is still in its infancy.

What's the answer to the constant funding struggle? The answer is eternal vigilance, raising public awareness—and therefore demand—through careful media and promotional activities and, importantly, through education and research. Although one of the principles upon which the program is based is that we train nonphysicians to be the advance care planning facilitators, educating doctors about the concept, the ethical and clinical importance, and the practicalities of advance care planning is essential to its ultimate success. It is for this reason that research is a mainstay of progress.

So where are we now? Thankfully, the stories that I recounted at the beginning of the chapter are now becoming the exception rather than the norm. To achieve a culture change in clinical practice takes time. On reflection, for the first few years, we have been consumed by building the evidence and with implementation of advance care planning. Although small by U.S. standards, we recognize that we need strategies to "sell the product" to more than 20 million Australians. We can't possibly do this without getting major buy-in from the mainstream health industry. The best way we can do that is by conducting the research that the health professionals take notice of. We began our research program seriously in 2007 by undertaking our randomized controlled trial of advance care planning in medical inpatients aged 80 or over. This was published as a landmark article in the *British Medical Journal* in March 2010.[1] The study showed that a systematized model of advance care planning, following the principles established by Respecting Choices, could significantly improve patient and family satisfaction regarding care; improve the knowledge of and respect for patients' end-of-life wishes; contribute to the quality of end-of-life care; and reduce the incidence of clinically significant anxiety, depression, and posttraumatic stress disorder in the surviving relatives of deceased patients. The impact of that publication has been greater than we anticipated. We are now undertaking research in multiple related research areas, and we are regarding our role as a Centre of Excellence.

Promotion of the advance care planning cause has also been conducted through our Web site (http://www.RespectingPatientChoices.org.au) and the vehicles of the International Society of Advance Care Planning and End of Life Care (http://www.acpel.com.au) and the society's international conferences. After the success of the first two conferences (Melbourne, April 2010, and London, June 2011), we look forward to the next conference in Chicago in June 2012.

For me, all this started when I saw a problem in the quality of care that we provide to critically ill patients and wanted to do something about it. I had no idea where that quest would take me, but I have enjoyed the journey immensely so far, and it's a long way from being over! And, if Dr. Bud Hammes had not answered his pager at Gundersen Health System one afternoon to take an overseas phone call from an unknown doctor with an Australian accent, the journey may have never been started. It also goes without saying that the journey would not have been as successful if not for the many dedicated people who are like-minded and have deep concern for the care that they provide to their patients with advanced illness.

Associate Professor William Silvester is a senior intensive care specialist at the Austin Hospital in Melbourne, in the Australian state of Victoria; the national director of the Respecting Patient Choices program in Australia; and the president of the International Society of Advance Care Planning and End of Life Care.

He gained his medical degree at the University of Western Australia and then trained as an internal medicine specialist, then in critical care medicine, in Perth, Western Australia. After three years overseas, including two years' research in intensive care in Britain, he returned to Australia.

Dr. Silvester is also a medical consultant for LifeGift, the Victorian Organ Donation Agency, and is chair of the Australian and New Zealand Intensive Care Society's Death and Organ Donation Committee and the society's End of Life Care Working Party.

Reference

1. Detering KM, Hancock AD, Reade MC, Silvester W. The impact of advance care planning on end of life care in elderly patients: randomised controlled trial. *BMJ*. 2010;340:c1345.

Section II

More Care and Support
Lead to Better Decisions

OVER THE PAST 40 years, medical science has fundamentally changed the course and experience of illnesses. Most of us will die at an older age from a chronic illness that progressively gets worse over a few to many years. This presents new challenges for people with such illnesses, for their families, and for the health system that cares for them.

Our health delivery system is not well designed to care for patients with chronic illness, especially in the advanced stages. This is not a criticism of any health professional or health system. We should recognize that our health system provides remarkable care of serious, life-threatening episodes of illness; prevents or delays many illnesses; and repairs a wide range of injuries. We clearly do NOT want to abandon or even weaken these services or the systems that deliver them.

With the success of our current health system clearly in mind, what we need to recognize is that the system today is not well designed to care for patients with advanced illness. It does not provide the best service to this group of patients and often does not fully understand what the patient wants or needs. Our current approaches to care often use some of the most expensive resources, which can both bankrupt the patient and undermine the ability of our communities to pay for health services.

In this section five authors will talk about new models of care that help persons with advanced illness live better (and, in many cases, longer), using less expensive resources to achieve this higher quality. These new approaches for caring for people with advanced illness have worked in different regions of the country and with diverse populations. This provides clear and promising examples of how we can refine our health system to better serve this growing vulnerable population. These new approaches don't replace or change what is currently working in our healthcare system; rather, they provide highly specialized care for this population of patients, just as we have specialized care for children and for expectant mothers.

In chapter 6, R. Sean Morrison, MD, director of the National Palliative Care Research Center, and Diane Meier, MD, director of the Center to Advance Palliative Care, describe the new specialty of palliative medicine and care. This is a new branch of medicine that focuses on the comfort and best functioning of patients. Palliative medicine ensures that the comfort of patients with advanced illness is maintained even while they may continue their regular treatment. In chapter 7, Thomas Klemond, MD, palliative care specialist, describes how Gundersen Health System has further redesigned its delivery system to bring together complex advance care planning, care coordination, and palliative care into a new service called Advanced Disease Coordination. Next, in chapter 8, Brad Stuart, MD, chief medical officer of Sutter Care at Home, describes how the treatment of illness has changed over time and how Sutter's Advanced Illness Management has improved care and lowered the cost of care. Dr. Stuart explains how this model and the others in this section deal with the three different dimensions of fragmentation that undermine the quality of care, especially for patients with advanced illness. In chapter 9, Randall Krakauer, MD, national medical director at Aetna, and Wayne Rawlins, MD, national medical director for Racial and Ethnic Equality Initiatives at Aetna, describe how this insurance company improved care by expanding hospice benefits to many of its members while not requiring these members to give up any access to other treatment. Finally, in chapter 10, Michael Fleming, MD, chief medical officer of Amedisys, a large national home health agency, describes how a more comprehensive, coordinated model of care provides significant benefits to patients at a lower cost.

In these chapters, readers will be given a window on how different healthcare providers and payers have created innovative programs that lead to better care for persons who have advanced illness and their families. The models of care presented in these chapters are slightly different from one another, but each provides more person- and family-centered care over time, as well as better coordination among providers in all settings. They all provide for a high quality of healthcare for persons with advanced illness and have a lower burden of treatment (and, thus, often come at a lower cost to both the patient and the payer).

six

The Value of Palliative Care to Patient and Family Outcomes

—R. Sean Morrison, MD,
and Diane E. Meier, MD

THE ELIMINATION OF suffering and the cure of disease are the fundamental goals of medicine.[1] While medical advances have transformed previously fatal conditions such as cancer and heart disease into illnesses that people can live with for many years, they have not been accompanied by corresponding improvements in the quality of life for these patients and their families.[2] Living with a serious illness should not mean living in pain or experiencing symptoms such as shortness of breath, nausea, or fatigue. Yet, multiple studies over the past decade suggest that medical care for patients with serious illness is characterized by inadequately treated physical distress; fragmented care systems; poor communication between doctors, patients, and families; and enormous strains on family caregiver and support systems.[3] In this chapter, we discuss how palliative care teams improve outcomes for seriously ill patients and their families. Subsequently, in chapter 15 we address the fiscal impact of palliative care programs and the need to incorporate palliative care programs into new models of healthcare delivery.

What Is Palliative Care?

Palliative care is interdisciplinary medical care focused on relief of pain and other symptoms and support for best possible quality of life for patients with serious illness and their families. It is appropriate at the point of diagnosis of a serious illness and provides an extra layer of support for patients and families.[4] It differs from hospice in that it offers patients and their families treatments focused on improving quality of life while they are receiving life-prolonging and curative treatments.[3] Interdisciplinary palliative care teams assess and treat symptoms, support decision making and help match treatments to informed patient and family goals, mobilize practical aid for patients and their family caregivers, identify community resources to ensure a safe and secure living environment, and promote collaborative and seamless models of care across a range of care settings (i.e., hospital, home, and nursing home). Palliative care programs have been shown to reduce symptoms, improve doctor-patient-family communication and satisfaction with care, and enhance the efficiency and effectiveness of hospital services.[5-7] In the past five years alone, the number of palliative care programs has more than doubled.[8] This growth is in response to the increasing numbers and needs of Americans living with serious, complex, and chronic illnesses and the realities of the care responsibilities faced by their families.

Distinguishing Palliative Care from Hospice Care

Although sometimes incorrectly linked to hospice in the minds of professionals and policy makers, palliative care is a distinct interdisciplinary specialty with considerably broader applicability. Hospice services in the United States are delivered in a model established by statute in Medicare and are followed by most other insurers and Medicaid. The Medicare hospice benefit is largely restricted to patients with a prognosis of living for six months or fewer, if the disease follows its natural course, and who agree to forgo therapies with curative intent. Hospice care is appropriate when patients and their families decide to forgo curative therapies in order to focus on maximizing comfort and quality of life, when curative treatments are no longer beneficial, when the burdens of these treatments outweigh their benefits, or when patients are entering the last weeks or months of life. Hospice services are highly standardized by the Medicare Conditions of Participation, although the intensity and nature of those services are determined by patient and family need and stage of illness (e.g., hospice services are typically most intensive in the last days of life, when symptoms and family distress often peak).[3,4,9] Hospice supports the family caregiver(s) throughout the care process and provides bereavement services to family members after the patient's death. In essence, hospice ensures high-quality medical care for patients and families at the end of life and through the dying and bereavement processes.

Disease-Directed Therapies

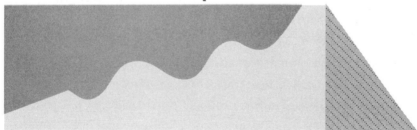

Diagnosis   Palliative Care

Conversely, palliative care is offered independent of the patient's prognosis and simultaneously with life-prolonging and curative therapies for a person living with serious, complex, and life-threatening illness (Figure 1). Ideally, palliative care should be initiated concurrently with a diagnosis of a serious illness and at the same time as curative or disease-modifying treatments, given the near-universal occurrence of patient and family distress and their need for information and support in establishing achievable goals for the patient's medical care. Unlike hospice, palliative care may be primary, secondary, or tertiary.[10] Primary palliative care should be part of what all treating clinicians provide their patients (such as pain and symptom management, discussions about advance care planning), secondary palliative care is offered when the treating physician refers to specialist-level palliative care experts for unusually complex or difficult problems, and tertiary palliative care includes research and teaching in addition to specialist-level palliative care expertise.

The Need for Palliative Care

Improvements in public health, the discovery of antibiotics, and advances in modern medicine have resulted in unprecedented gains in human longevity. Eventually, however, most adults will develop one or more chronic illnesses with which they will live for years before death,[3] and tragically, more than 25,000 children per year in the United States are born with or develop a serious or life-threatening disease, such as cancer, cystic fibrosis, cerebral palsy, or muscular dystrophy.[11] For both adults and children, the years following diagnosis are characterized by physical and psychological symptom distress, progressive functional dependence and frailty, and high family support needs. These patients and families confront a U.S. healthcare system organized around specialists who are focused on acute (and narrow) episodes of care and who feel pressure to see more patients in less time. Ample evidence demonstrates that patients with serious illness experience a multitude of profoundly distressing symptoms that devastate them and consume their families. A conservative estimate suggests that of the one million persons who died in a U.S. hospital in 2001, 324,000 had fatigue, 280,000 had loss of appetite, 244,000 had shortness of breath, 232,000 had dry mouth and oral ulcers, 208,000 had cough, 196,000 had pain, 148,000 had confusion, 148,000 had depression, 140,000 had nausea, 92,000 had difficulty sleeping, and 88,000 had vomiting.[12] The reasons for this distressing state of affairs are many, but almost all stem from a philosophy of healthcare that has traditionally viewed symptoms and suffering as unimportant and interesting only insofar as they guide the physician to a correct diagnosis. The prevailing philosophy dictates that once the diagnosis is made (e.g., cancer) and the disease is treated (e.g., chemotherapy), the symptoms (e.g., breathlessness, pain) will dissipate. This philosophy ignores the reality that some disease-directed treatments may be ineffective—particularly in advanced disease—and that the presence of distressing symptoms in and of themselves leads to reduced quality of life, adverse outcomes, and increased costs.[12]

Skilled communication is one of the cornerstones of appropriate care for persons with serious illness. Healthcare professionals are commonly called upon to deliver bad news to patients (e.g., a diagnosis of cancer, a diagnosis of amyotrophic lateral sclerosis [ALS]), discuss goals of care (e.g., what treatments meet the values and goals of the individual patient and his or her family), and make complicated and difficult treatment decisions (e.g., decisions to stop treatments, such as chemotherapy or mechanical ventilation, that no longer meet treatment goals, decisions to enroll in experimental protocols). Abundant research demonstrates that physicians are uncomfortable having these discussions and infrequently engage in them and that when they do, they rarely perform them in a manner that is patient centered rather than physician centered or that meets the expressed needs of patients and families. Indeed, most patients report being dissatisfied with how physicians communicate bad news or explain treatment decisions. A major reason for these findings is that clinicians are not trained in the critical skills of communication and rarely have such skills modeled for them.

Finally, it is also clear that our current systems of care and reimbursement fail to address many of the needs of patients with serious illness. Medicare is targeted to acute, episodic illness and is not well equipped to respond to the long-term needs of the chronically ill. Medicare covers acute hospitalizations, physician services, rehabilitation, and short-term posthospital care. Since 1983, the Medicare hospice benefit also provides care to dying patients or those near the very end of life. It is the minority of people with serious illness—limited to a subset of those with predictable prognoses—who can benefit from this system.

For example, the typical patient diagnosed with metastatic colon cancer will enjoy a relatively stable period of good functional status followed by a predictable and rapid period of functional decline before death. This person can be well served by traditional Medicare during his or her time of stable health and by the Medicare hospice benefit during the short period of disability prior to death. However, the vast majority of patients with serious and chronic illness have uncertain life prognoses; have poorly predictable disease trajectories; and require care beyond that typically provided by acute care hospitals, physician office visits, and hospice. These patients make multiple transitions between care settings and require long-term care at home or in skilled nursing facilities, care coordination as they traverse a fragmented system, personal (bathing, dressing, toileting) and custodial (shopping, housekeeping, laundry) care needs, home infusion therapies, and transportation to physicians' offices and other healthcare settings—most of which remain uncovered by Medicare and third-party payers. Successful care of persons with serious illness will require the development of palliative care programs that can address symptoms (physical, psychological, spiritual), communication, and family needs across all healthcare settings.

Essential Elements of Quality Palliative Care

As outlined by the National Quality Forum (NQF),[4] the National Consensus Project for Quality Palliative Care,[9] and the Joint Commission,[13] the essential structural elements of palliative care are

- An interdisciplinary team of clinical staff (physician, nurse, social worker, spiritual counselor, pharmacist, aide, volunteers);
- Staffing ratios determined by the nature and size of the population to be served;
- Staff trained, credentialed, and/or certified in palliative care; and
- Access and responsiveness 24 hours per day, 7 days per week.

The NQF Guidelines[4] include 38 preferred structure and quality practices (http://www.capc.org/tools-for-palliative-care-programs/national-guidelines/) that have been used to develop quality metrics for hospital palliative care services in the United States.[14-18] Examples of preferred practice measures are the determination and documentation of patient and family goals for care through advance care planning, using, for example, the Medical or Physician Orders for Life-Sustaining Treatment (also known as MOLST or POLST; see http://www.polst.org)[19,20] or the Respecting Choices paradigm (http://www.respectingchoices.org),[21] both of which have been shown to increase the likelihood that the care actually received is concordant with the patient's goals. Palliative care programs within Joint Commission–accredited hospitals that meet the following criteria are eligible for Advanced Certification for Palliative Care under a newly established Joint Commission program[13]:

- Provide the full range of palliative care services to hospitalized patients 24 hours per day, 7 days per week;
- Have served a minimum of 10 patients and have at least 1 active patient at the time of the initial Joint Commission on-site review;
- Use a standardized method of delivering clinical care based on clinical practice guidelines and/or evidence-based practice;
- Have the ability to direct the clinical management of patients and coordinate care (such as write orders, direct or coordinate activities of the program team, and influence composition of the program team);
- Follow an organized approach supported by an interdisciplinary team of health professionals; and
- Use performance measurement to improve performance over time.

The Effect of Palliative Care
on Patient and Family Outcomes

Palliative care teams demonstrably improve physical and psychosocial symptoms; family caregiver well-being; bereavement outcomes; and patient, family, and physician satisfaction.[5,22-37] These objectives are achieved through care provided by interdisciplinary teams of physicians, nurses, social workers, spiritual counselors, pharmacists, aides, and additional personnel as needed (physical therapists, psychologists, and others). Palliative care teams identify and rapidly treat distressing symptoms that have been independently shown to increase medical complications and hospitalization.[25,32,38] Palliative care teams meet often with patients and their families to establish appropriate and realistic goals, support families in crisis, and plan for safe transitions out of hospitals to more supportive settings (home care, home hospice, nursing home care with hospice, or inpatient hospice care). Communication regarding the patient's prognosis and goals by a dedicated team with time and expertise leads to better-informed decision making, clarity of the care plan, and consistent follow through. Such discussions at family meetings lead to lower costs and a lighter family burden[36,37] and improve family satisfaction and bereavement outcomes.[33,36]

Finally, and contrary to widely held assumptions, one recent study suggests that palliative care may be associated with a significant *prolongation* of life.[5] Research is necessary to confirm these findings and assess their generalizability. Conjectures accounting for the possibility that palliative care may prolong life include reduction in depression, which is an independent predictor of mortality in multiple disease types; avoidance of the hazards of hospitalization and high-risk medical interventions; reduction in symptom burden; and improved support for family caregivers that permits patients to remain safely at home.

Care for persons with serious illness and their families needs improvement. Untreated physical symptoms, poor communication between providers and patients, and treatment decisions in conflict with patient and family preferences characterize the current standard of healthcare for our sickest and most vulnerable patients. Surveys of patients and their families have identified relief of suffering, practical support needs, open communication, and opportunities to relieve burdens on and strengthen relationships with family as the top priority needs from the healthcare system. The field of palliative care was developed in direct response to the unmet needs and wishes of patients and their families, and the early success of the field has been remarkable. However, truly transforming the care of persons with serious illness and ensuring access to high-quality palliative care for all Americans who might benefit require that providers be trained to deliver this kind of care, that an evidence base exist to ensure quality, that healthcare organizations have the capacity to provide it, and that the public understand palliative care and demand such care from their clinicians. We have come a long way toward achieving these goals. The next step is to ensure that palliative care is completely integrated into our current healthcare system, as described in chapter 15.

R. Sean Morrison, MD, is director of the National Palliative Care Research Center, a national organization devoted to increasing the evidence base of palliative care in the United States. He is also the vice chair of research, professor of geriatrics and medicine, and Hermann Merkin Professor of Palliative Medicine in the Brookdale Department of Geriatrics and Palliative Medicine at the Mount Sinai School of Medicine in New York City. During 2009–2010, he served as president of the American Academy of Hospice and Palliative Medicine.

Dr. Morrison is the recipient of numerous awards, including a PDIA American Academy of Hospice and Palliative Medicine National Leadership Award, the American Geriatrics Society's Outstanding Achievement for Clinical Investigation Award, the Open Society Institute Faculty Scholar's Award of the Project on Death in America, a Paul Beeson Faculty Scholars Award, a Brookdale National Fellowship, and a Faculty Council Award from the Mount Sinai School of Medicine. He is currently principal investigator of an NIA-funded five-year multisite study on improving the management of pain in older adults.

Dr. Morrison has received more than \$35 million in research funding and published more than 100 research articles. His work has appeared in all major peer-reviewed medical journals, including the *New England Journal of Medicine*, *Annals of Internal Medicine*, and the *Journal of the American Medical Association*. He edited the first textbook on geriatric palliative care and has contributed to more than 15 books on the subjects of geriatrics and palliative care. As one of the leading figures in the field of palliative medicine, Dr. Morrison has appeared numerous times on television and in print, including *ABC World News Tonight*, *The Factor with Bill O'Reilly*, *The New York Times*, the *Los Angeles Times*, *USA Today*, the *Philadelphia Enquirer*, the *New York Daily News*, *Newsday*, *AARP*, and *Newsweek*. He figured prominently in the Bill Moyers series *On Our Own Terms*, a four-part documentary aired on PBS, and in Gail Sheehy's new book, *Passages in Caregiving*.

Dr. Morrison received his BA from Brown University and his MD from the University of Chicago Pritzker School of Medicine. He completed his residency training at the New York Hospital–Cornell Medical Center, followed by fellowship training at the Mount Sinai School of Medicine in New York City. He has been on the faculty of the Department of Geriatrics and Palliative Medicine and Department of Medicine at Mount Sinai since 1995.

Diane E. Meier, MD, is director of the Center to Advance Palliative Care (CAPC), a national organization devoted to increasing the number and quality of palliative care programs in the United States. Under her leadership, the number of palliative care programs in U.S. hospitals has more than doubled in the past five years. She is also director of the Lilian and Benjamin Hertzberg Palliative Care Institute, professor of geriatrics and internal medicine, and Catherine Gaisman Professor of Medical Ethics at Mount Sinai School of Medicine in New York City.

Dr. Meier was named one of "20 People Who Make Healthcare Better" in the United States by HealthLeaders Media 2010. She received a MacArthur Foundation Fellowship in September of 2008 and an Honorary Doctorate of Science from Oberlin College in 2010. Other honors include the Open Society Institute Faculty Scholar's Award of the Project on Death in America, the Alexander Richman Commemorative Award for Humanism in Medicine, the Founders Award of the National Hospice and Palliative Care Organization 2007, the AARP 50th Anniversary Social Impact Award 2008, Gold Humanism Honor Society National Honoree 2008, Castle Connelly's Physician of the Year Award 2009, and the American Academy of Hospice and Palliative Medicine Lifetime Achievement Award 2009. She is currently principal investigator of an NCI-funded five-year multisite study on the outcomes of hospital palliative care services in cancer patients. Dr. Meier served as one of Columbia University's Health and Aging Policy Fellows in Washington, DC, during the 2009–2010 academic year, working on both the Senate's HELP Committee and the Department of Health and Human Services.

Dr. Meier has published extensively in all major peer-reviewed medical journals, including the *New England Journal of Medicine* and the *Journal of the American Medical Association*. Her most recent book, *Palliative Care: Transforming the Care of Serious Illness*, was published by Jossey in 2010. She edited the first textbook on geriatric palliative care, as well as four editions of *Geriatric Medicine*. As one of the leading figures in the field of palliative medicine, Dr. Meier has appeared numerous times on television and in print, including *ABC World News Tonight*, *Open Mind with Richard Hefner*, *The New York Times*, the *Los Angeles Times*, *USA Today*, the *New York Daily News*, *Newsday*, *The New Yorker*, *AARP*, and *Newsweek*. She figured prominently in the Bill Moyers series *On Our Own Terms*, a four-part documentary aired on PBS.

Dr. Meier received her BA from Oberlin College and her MD from Northwestern University Medical School. She completed her residency and fellowship training at Oregon Health Sciences University in Portland. She has been on the faculty of the Department of Geriatrics and Adult Development and Department of Medicine at Mount Sinai since 1983.

References

1. Cassel EJ. The nature of suffering and the goals of medicine. *New England Journal of Medicine.* 1982;306(11):639-45.

2. The SUPPORT Investigators. A controlled trial to improve care for seriously ill hospitalized patients: the study to understand prognoses and preferences for outcomes and risks of treatments (SUPPORT). *JAMA: Journal of the American Medical Association.* 1995;274(20):22-29.

3. Morrison RS, Meier DE. Clinical practice: palliative care. *New England Journal of Medicine.* 2004;350(25):2582-2590.

4. National Quality Forum. *A national framework and preferred practices for palliative and hospice care quality.* Washington, DC: National Quality Forum; 2006.

5. Temel JS, Greer JA, Muzikansky A, et al. Early palliative care for patients with metastatic non-small-cell lung cancer. *New England Journal of Medicine.* 2010;363(8):733-742.

6. Morrison RS, Cassel JB, Caust-Ellenbogen M, Spragens L, Meier DE. Substantial cost savings associated with hospital-based palliative care programs. *Journal of the American Geriatrics Society.* 2007;44(S1):S7.

7. Gelfman LP, Meier DE, Morrison RS. Does palliative care improve quality? A survey of bereaved family members. *Journal of Pain and Symptom Management.* 2008;36(1):22-28.

8. Goldsmith B, Dietrich J, Du Q, Morrison RS. Variability in access to hospital palliative care in the United States. *Journal of Palliative Medicine.* 2008;11(8):1094-1102.

9. National Consensus Project for Quality Palliative Care. *Clinical practice guidelines for quality palliative care.* New York: National Consensus Project for Quality Palliative Care; 2004.

10. von Gunten CF. Secondary and tertiary palliative care in US hospitals. *JAMA: Journal of the American Medical Association.* 2002;287(7):875-881.

11. Friebert SM. NHPCO facts and figures: pediatric palliative and hospice care in America. http://www.nhpco.org/files/public/quality/Pediatric_Facts-Figures.pdf. Accessed October 14, 2011.

12. von Gunten CF. Interventions to manage symptoms at the end of life. *Journal of Palliative Medicine.* 2005;8(Suppl 1):S88-S94.

13. Joint Commission. Advanced certification for palliative care programs: disease specific certification. http://www.jointcommission.org/certification/palliative_care.aspx. Accessed August 30, 2011.

14. Arnold RM, Weissman DE. Broaching the topic of a palliative care consultation with patients and families #42. *Journal of Palliative Medicine.* 2004;7(3):472-473.

15. Weissman DE, Morrison RS, Meier DE. Center to Advance Palliative Care palliative care clinical care and customer satisfaction metrics consensus recommendations. *Journal of Palliative Medicine.* 2010;13(2):179-84.

16. Weissman DE, Meier DE, Spragens LH. Center to Advance Palliative Care palliative care consultation service metrics: consensus recommendations. *Journal of Palliative Medicine.* 2008;11(10):1294-1298.

17. Weissman DE, Meier DE. Center to Advance Palliative Care inpatient unit operational metrics: consensus recommendations. *Journal of Palliative Medicine.* 2009;12(1):21-25.

18. Weissman DE, Meier DE. Operational features for hospital palliative care programs: consensus recommendations. *Journal of Palliative Medicine.* 2008;11(9):1189-1194.

19. Hickman SE, Nelson CA, Perrin NA, Moss AH, Hammes BJ, Tolle SW. A comparison of methods to communicate treatment preferences in nursing facilities: traditional practices versus the Physician Orders for Life-Sustaining Treatment program. *Journal of the American Geriatrics Society.* 2010;58(7):1241-1248.

20. Meier DE, Beresford L. POLST offers next stage in honoring patient preferences. *Journal of Palliative Medicine.* 2009;12(4):291-295.

21. Hammes BJ, Rooney BL, Gundrum JD. A comparative, retrospective, observational study of the prevalence, availability, and specificity of advance care plans in a county that implemented an advance care planning microsystem. *Journal of the American Geriatrics Society.* 2010;58(7):1249-1255.

22. Cassel JB, Smith TJ, Coyne PJ, Hager MA, Baker SJ. A high volume, specialist, standardized care palliative care unit generates revenue sufficient to cover end of life care costs. http://www.asco.org/ascov2/Meetings/ Abstracts?&vmview=abst_detail_view&confID=16&abstractID=1412. Accessed October 14, 2011.

23. Casarett D, Pickard A, Bailey FA, et al. Do palliative consultations improve patient outcomes? *Journal of the American Geriatrics Society.* 2008;56(4):593-599.

24. Rabow MW, Petersen J, Schanche K, Dibble SL, McPhee SJ. The comprehensive care team: a description of a controlled trial of care at the beginning of the end of life. *Journal of Palliative Medicine.* 2003;6(3):489-499.

25. Manfredi PL, Morrison RS, Morris J, Goldhirsch SL, Carter JM, Meier DE. Palliative care consultations: how do they impact the care of hospitalized patients? *Journal of Pain and Symptom Management.* 2000;20(3):166-173.

26. Jordhoy MS, Fayers P, Loge JH, Ahlner-Elmqvist M, Kaasa S. Quality of life in palliative cancer care: results from a cluster randomized trial. *Journal of Clinical Oncology.* 2001;19(18):3884-3894.

27. Ringdal GI, Jordhøy MS, Kaasa S. Family satisfaction with end-of-life care for cancer patients in a cluster randomized trial. *Journal of Pain and Symptom Management.* 2002;24(1):53-63.

28. Lilly CM, De Meo DL, Sonna LA, et al. An intensive communication intervention for the critically ill. *American Journal of Medicine.* 2000;109(6):469-475.

29. Fallowfield L, Jenkins V. Communicating sad, bad, and difficult news in medicine. *Lancet.* 2004;363(9405):312-319.

30. Elsayem A, Swint K, Fisch MJ, et al. Palliative care inpatient service in a comprehensive cancer center: clinical and financial outcomes. *Journal of Clinical Oncology.* 2004;22(10):2008-2014.

31. Fellowes D, Wilkinson S, Moore P. Communication skills training for health care professionals working with cancer patients, their families and/or carers. *Cochrane Database of Systematic Reviews.* 2004;(2):CD003751.

32. Jordhøy MS, Fayers P, Saltnes T, Ahlner-Elmqvist M, Jannert M, Kaasa S. A palliative-care intervention and death at home: a cluster randomised trial. *Lancet.* 2000;356(9233):888-893.

33. Zhang B, Wright AA, Huskamp HA, et al. Health care costs in the last week of life: associations with end-of-life conversations. *Archives of Internal Medicine.* 2009;169(5):480-488.

34. Teno JM, Clarridge BR, Casey V, et al. Family perspectives on end-of-life care at the last place of care. *JAMA: Journal of the American Medical Association.* 2004;291(1):88-93.

35. Nilsson ME, Maciejewski PK, Zhang B, et al. Mental health, treatment preferences, advance care planning, location, and quality of death in advanced cancer patients with dependent children. *Cancer.* 2009;115(2):399-409.

36. Wright AA, Zhang B, Ray A, et al. Associations between end-of-life discussions, patient mental health, medical care near death, and caregiver bereavement adjustment. *JAMA: Journal of the American Medical Association.* 2008;300(14):1665-1673.

37. Wright AA, Keating NL, Balboni TA, Matulonis UA, Block SD, Prigerson HG. Place of death: correlations with quality of life of patients with cancer and predictors of bereaved caregivers' mental health. *Journal of Clinical Oncology.* 2010;28(29):4457-4464.

38. Morrison RS, Flanagan S, Fischberg D, Cintron A, Siu AL. A novel interdisciplinary analgesic program reduces pain and improves function in older adults after orthopedic surgery. *Journal of the American Geriatrics Society.* 2009;57(1):1-10.

seven

Hope for the Future with a Human Touch: Advanced Disease Coordination

—Thomas Klemond, MD

I FIRST MET John in the hospital. He was a 64-year-old man with a worn-out heart and a liver that wasn't far behind. His blood pressure was so low that he could barely stand, and managing his many medications and other failing organs was a daily—sometimes hourly—medical challenge. He was neither interested in nor a candidate for a heart transplant, and he wanted no further heroic treatments. More than anything, he wanted to be out of the hospital and at peace. We talked at length about all of this in the hospital with John and his sister and then about providing him comfort and the best support we could, knowing that he would likely live only a short while. Unfortunately (although expected and normal for this stage of illness), he was too weak to go home and had to be placed in a nursing home.

The evening after his departure to the nursing home, I received a call from a frantic nurse that his blood pressure was very low and that he could "barely walk." I assured her that this was all expected, given his advanced disease state and that his wishes were not to be hospitalized. Together we reviewed his care plan and updated his family on his condition.

Three days later I received another frantic call from a nurse practitioner in the heart failure clinic, where John had been scheduled to follow up as a standard process. "[John's] blood pressure is very low, and he can barely even sit up! I think he needs to be in the hospital, maybe in intensive care!" I went to the heart failure clinic, and there was John, looking much as he had when I had discharged him from the hospital. We reaffirmed his wishes and made arrangements for him to go back to the nursing home. I called his sister to let her know that he was continuing to decline and that he likely had only a few days left to live.

John died peacefully three days later, with his family at his bedside at the nursing home. It was great care for John, and his family was very appreciative of it. But the quality care that was provided went largely unrecognized by others in the system and is poorly reimbursed by the current healthcare system.

Background

"We can't solve problems by using the same
kind of thinking we used when we created them."
—Albert Einstein

It should come as no surprise to readers that our healthcare system as configured is financially unsustainable. There are many contributing factors to this, including the third-party reimbursement system, the aging of the baby boomers, and the frequent well-intended but blind embrace of expensive treatments that may offer marginal or no benefit. Fortunately, from a clinical standpoint, many financial outlays occur more as a result of two factors: (1) a lack of cohesiveness of the care provided in the setting of advanced illness and (2) a societal uncertainty about how to deal with the reality of advanced illness in an age when medical science is often promoted as able to treat and cure every illness.[1]

Patients and families progressing through advanced chronic illness face the challenges of physical decline, loss of independence, and grappling with death, while at the same time they make their way through an increasingly complex, fragmented, and sometimes dangerous healthcare system. The system, which has developed in response to a reimbursement model that rewards intervention and avoidance of death at all cost, almost certainly at some point in the course of every illness causes suffering—both by the pain and hardship of the interventions and by the hiding or neglect of the reality of death and the important human work of dying.[2,3]

Improving care in the current healthcare climate will require a new way of looking at, providing, and financially supporting the care provided. Critical attributes of the new care model will be that it must improve the coordination of care and it must promote care decisions and the provision of subsequent care with a shared acknowledgment of the inevitability and approach of death. While this awareness commonly and rightly changes the priorities of patients and families, without effective coordination of subsequent care, these priorities can be neglected as the system provides usual care and usual responses to circumstances. Furthermore, the awareness and eventual acceptance of death occur most often over time and are therefore best served by ongoing conversation and collaboration with people who know you well. Decisions coming from this partnership should build on or start from earlier expressed goals and apply them, along with changing perspective, to evolving clinical circumstances.

Gundersen Health System and Advanced Chronic Illness: Evolution of a New Paradigm

There is substantial ongoing national attention to these challenges. Many programs are developing in an attempt to redesign care to better serve the patients and circumstances common to advanced illness. There is also a recognition that the current healthcare system, in addition to being prohibitively expensive, frequently leads to dissatisfaction in patients with advanced illness.[4,5] Given the structure and limitations of the current system, a compelling concept put forward has been to utilize hospitals and acute care settings to provide ongoing care in advanced chronic illness.[6] The medical home and accountable care organization movements have also developed with the aim of improving care by redesigning the system of care delivery.

While improving coordination and continuity of care across settings (e.g., from the doctor's office, to the emergency department, to the hospital, to the nursing home) is a critical part of a sustainable model of care, the element of communication related to end-of-life care is habitually missing from developmental models. Without honest and ongoing patient-centered dialogue about declining health and function and the common circumstances of advanced illness, acute care decisions will continue to be made somewhat blindly by providers and patients.

At Gundersen Health System, an innovative program has been developed over the past decade in response to these challenges. In our efforts to improve the care of our patients, as well as offer insight and assist the national dialogue on healthcare reform, we have identified and linked three high-quality supportive services related to advanced chronic illness: advance care planning, care coordination, and palliative care.

Advance Care Planning

While discussed in detail elsewhere in this book, advance care planning, or the process of making one's wishes known related to healthcare in dire circumstances, is most often a fundamentally positive intervention for patients, families, and providers. This communication, which should be something we all participate in over the course of our lives, is of critical importance in hospitals and emergency rooms, where the planned-for circumstances inevitably come to pass. Without them, decisions must be made by family members and doctors, who often don't have the level of insight needed to act in accordance with the patient's goals and wishes.

I have been a Gundersen Health System clinician over the past 12 years and have seen that the advance care planning integrated into our local culture has literally "moved the floor" from which my patients and I make medical decisions. By this I mean that when I meet patients with advanced illness for the first time, the dialogue often begins at a point that in other communities is reached later in the course of illness, if at all. Patient wishes regarding cardiopulmonary resuscitation (CPR), nursing homes, feeding tubes, and even organ donation have already been expressed, so the dialogue can move quickly and effectively into the present circumstances.

While this local cultural norm is helpful in providing the right care for all patients, the dialogue about goals and care in patients with advanced illness is best seen as an ongoing conversation. In this regard, since the early 2000s, Gundersen Health System has been developing a new advance care planning intervention, one that is more in-depth and focused on advanced chronic illness. This tool, locally called the "Next Steps Conversation," has been tested and proven to better prepare patients, families, and providers to face the circumstances of advanced chronic illness. When patients and families are involved in the discussion and when realistic scenarios common to serious illness are evaluated, a more detailed description of patient goals is developed. This conversation, which draws from the initial advance care planning work recommended for the general public, forms part of the initial establishment of a relationship with persons with advanced illness. As such, it serves to help educate, set expectations, and guide the subsequent supportive care system.

Care Coordination

Care coordination at Gundersen Health System is a nursing initiative that has dramatically improved the quality of care while reducing resource utilization. The program, developed in 2001, is currently staffed by more than 20 nurses who have an average of 27 years of experience, along with social services support. The model involves assigning a group of medically complex patients to a specific nurse or "care coordinator," who, along with a social worker, serves as a coach and guide through the healthcare system. This program has dramatically improved the care of these patients and resulted in higher patient satisfaction and quality-of-life scores while reducing average annual medical costs by more than $15,000 per patient per year.[7] A central principle of the care coordination program is that every patient with advanced chronic illness needs a nurse advocate. Conceptually, this role can also be fulfilled by a hospice nurse, nursing home charge nurse, or other nurse navigator, but the care coordination model has been utilized most extensively in program development. It should be noted that the role can be and sometimes is transferred from one nurse to another (e.g., a care coordinator hands off to a hospice nurse as the patient transitions to comfort-focused care).

The nurse advocate is connected to the patient, has a good working knowledge of the healthcare system being utilized, and has good access to provider support. The U.S. healthcare system is highly fragmented at the provider level, both by organ system (e.g., heart specialist, kidney specialist) and by acuity (i.e., providers usually work only in medical clinics, emergency departments, or hospitals). Without accompaniment with and oversight from an experienced person who is oriented to and familiar with the patient, the resulting fragmentation can lead to providers making decisions about care with limited information and with a systemic bias toward treatment and intervention. In general, the experienced nurse is the least expensive, most available, and most appropriately qualified person to play this role, as long as provider oversight is readily available.

Palliative Care

Palliative care is a medical subspecialty and a philosophy of care dedicated to the relief of suffering. As a field, it has grown rapidly in the past decade, mostly in the hospital setting. By focusing on patients and their symptoms, rather than the organ or the disease process, palliative care in the United States is most commonly offered simultaneously with regular medical care, usually playing an increasing role in care as patients reach late life and terminal illness. As patients progress with advanced illness, their comfort and relief of suffering most often become higher priorities than treatments aimed at sustaining physiologic life.

Palliative care teams spend more time with patients and families than do traditional medical teams, and they have expertise in managing the symptoms and circumstances common to advanced chronic illness. In general, palliative care services improve patient and family satisfaction with care while reducing the cost of care, although the latter is not the goal or intent of palliative care. It is rather the more frequent result of honest and frank discussions regarding illness in a medical environment that inherently favors aggressive treatment at all stages of illness, including in dying patients.

The Gundersen Health System palliative care service was established in 1997 and has provided care for thousands of patients and families over the past 14 years. As with most programs nationwide, our service was developed by clinicians and others within our healthcare system (with assistance from national centers such as the Center to Advance Palliative Care) in response to the suffering seen in patients with advanced illness and their families. The program has been well supported within our institution by patients, providers, and administration. In 2010, more than 60% of the patients who died at our facility did so with the palliative care team involved in their care. Families of these patients report levels of satisfaction with all aspects of care equal to or higher than those of families of patients not seen by palliative care.

While the role of palliative care in hospitals is well established, the reality of chronic illness is that death is sometimes unpredictable and most often takes place over weeks or months. This, from our experience, has sometimes challenged the effectiveness of hospital-based palliative involvement, as hospitalizations are usually relatively brief. In response to this, over the past five years our palliative service has expanded its role in patient care to provide more longitudinal support in the outpatient setting.

Putting It All Together:
Advanced Disease Coordination

The merging of these three elements of care has resulted in the establishment of a new model of supportive care that we call "advanced disease coordination," or ADC. This service model, which is designed to establish and maintain relationships with patients and families in the final months to years of life, utilizes the strengths of advance care planning, coordination of care, and palliative care.

Patients are referred to the program by their primary care providers or key specialists (such as oncologists for cancer patients) when they reach an advanced stage of illness but may still be undergoing aggressive life-sustaining or prolonging treatment. Patients and families meet the care team, composed of care coordination nurses, palliative providers, social workers, and chaplains, and through a series of meetings a care plan is developed and a supportive relationship established. Subsequent care is provided by primary care providers and the ADC team, in collaboration with other involved medical teams. Patients and families are given high-quality 24-hour access to the ADC team and are seen in the clinic setting as needed to help with symptoms and other challenging circumstances. It has been a priority of the outpatient team to appreciate and strengthen, rather than replace, the existing primary care and other involved provider roles. This emphasis carries over into the hospital setting, as well, where outpatient healthcare relationships are seldom recognized or utilized in care decisions, despite the fact that positive outcomes have been associated with involvement of outpatient providers in inpatient events.[8]

When enrolled patients are ill or need emergency care, they are seen by the ADC acute care team, along with other appropriate medical providers. The acute care team, composed of a palliative physician and nurse practitioner, coordinates appropriate care in collaboration with subspecialists, surgeons, and other providers in our system, and the result is the provision of high-quality care that is consistent with patient goals and wishes. Patients' priorities can change as their diseases progress; while in the early stages of advanced illness, they most frequently desire aggressive life-sustaining care, but over time and with disease progression, they often begin to put a higher value on independence, comfort, and "not being a burden" more than on prolonging organ function for as long as possible. From here, as patients reach the end stages of illness, relief of pain, breathlessness, and other distressing symptoms becomes the highest priority. The ADC team maintains a relationship with patients and families through this process, a practice we describe as "walking with them." While these stages are common to advanced illness, each patient and family is unique, and the care provided is "custom fit" to each circumstance, guided by the relationship established and prior conversations about goals.

The ADC program was developed at our facility over the past five years and became operational in its mature form in February of 2010. It has been well received by patients, families, and other providers, particularly in the acute care setting; with endorsement from primary care providers and key subspecialists, nearly 100% of patients offered the service have enrolled. Quality and outcome data are being measured and will guide subsequent utilization. The program has been developed in conjunction with the Centers for Medicare and Medicaid Services as a demonstration project.

Challenges and Future Directions

There have been many challenges faced in development and operation of the service: Treatments are readily available at nearly every stage of illness, and likely outcomes are often not clear when decisions regarding care must be made. Patients feel pressure to continue treatment in this setting and sometimes fear the stigma of "giving up" or letting down family members or even providers. Additionally, ongoing treatments might obscure the truth of decline and dying, by leaving patients and families with little time or opportunity to do the important tasks of reconciliation or even saying good-bye.[9] Doctors are trained to cure and often fear expressing doubt about whether their patients will survive, which further hinders progress toward dying in peace. Yet another formidable challenge is the unavoidable truth that usually we are weak in the last weeks to months of life, sometimes to the point of needing assistance day and night with the basic tasks of living. With a nearly universal societal norm that nursing homes are to be avoided at all costs, patients, families, and the healthcare system struggle to support this goal.

We do not yet have—and perhaps we may never have—specific answers to these challenges, many of which are consequences of our own development as a society. But the creation and financial reimbursement of supportive care systems like advanced disease coordination is the right next step in uniting patients, providers, and the healthcare system as we face together the many challenges of advanced chronic illness. It is our hope that this patient-centered model of care will become the norm rather than the exception to how healthcare is provided for ourselves, our families, and our communities.

Thomas Klemond, MD, received his undergraduate degree and medical training at the University of Minnesota, with residency training and board certification in internal medicine completed at Gundersen Health System in 2002. He has worked as a hospitalist and palliative physician at Gundersen since that time and attained board certification in hospice and palliative medicine in 2006. His program development experience includes work in developing the hospitalist and palliative programs at Gundersen. Besides being involved full-time in the care of patients with advanced and often terminal illness, he is coauthor of the Gundersen Health System Medicare Demonstration Project 646. The demonstration, known locally as advanced disease coordination, was approved and initiated in February of 2010 and involves the creation and implementation of an innovative service model that integrates high-quality advance care planning, care coordination, and palliative care with the intent of improving the quality of care for patients with advanced illness and their families.

References

1. Becker E. *The denial of death*. New York: Free Press; 1973.

2. Byock I. *Dying well: the prospect for growth at the end of life*. New York: Riverhead Books; 1997.

3. Kübler-Ross E. *On death and dying*. New York: Macmillan; 1969.

4. Boyd CM, Darer J, Boult C, Fried LP, Boult L, Wu AW. Clinical practice guidelines and quality of care for older patients with multiple comorbid diseases: implications for pay for performance. *JAMA: Journal of the American Medical Association*. 2005;294(6):716-724.

5. Shadmi E, Boyd CM, Hsiao CJ, Sylvia M, Schuster AB, Boult C. Morbidity and older persons' perceptions of the quality of their primary care. *Journal of the American Geriatrics Society*. 2006;54(2):330-334.

6. Siu AL, Spragens LH, Inouye SK, Morrison RS, Leff B. The ironic business case for chronic care in the acute care setting. *Health Affairs (Millwood)*. 2009;28(1):113-125.

7. Bintz M, Tucker L, Lachman V, Bahr J, Larson D. Transformational patient care: a system of care coordination that works. *Group Practice Journal*. 2009;58(4):15.

8. Sharma G, Freeman J, Zhang D, Goodwin JS. Continuity of care and intensive care unit use at the end of life. *Archives of Internal Medicine*. 2009;169(1):81-86.

9. Hanson LC, Danis M, Garrett J. What is wrong with end-of-life care? Opinions of bereaved family members. *Journal of the American Geriatrics Society*. 1997;45(11):1339-1344.

eight

Advanced Care: Choice, Comfort, and Control for the Seriously Ill

—Brad Stuart, MD

LIKE HIS FATHER and grandfather before him, Chuck C. started in the coal mines of West Virginia at 14, worked 12-hour shifts, smoked two packs a day, and quit at 50 when he ran out of wind. He and his wife, Louise, retired to a trailer park in northern California on health insurance and a pension from the company. At 65 he became eligible for Medicare.

Chuck got around in a motorized scooter with an oxygen tank. Strapped to the back, sticking seven feet in the air, was a fly rod that bent in the breeze, an old coon tail flapping at the tip like a fresh-caught rainbow trout. Chuck hadn't really been fishing in years. His last trip ended when he slipped and fell on the rocks at the river's edge, which left him gasping for air like one of the fish in his creel. These days he spent more time in a hospital bed than out in the sun. He was admitted four or five times a year with pneumonia, and each stay was longer than the last.

Every time Chuck came home from the hospital, he seemed worse than when he went in. Weaker, more tired, and short of breath, he found that getting around became harder and harder. Louise strained her back when trying to move him from his bed to a chair. She couldn't get any sleep. She was at her wits' end trying to keep track of his pills. They changed every time he went to the hospital, and the doctors there never seemed to talk with Chuck's family doctor. Louise had to run all over town trying to figure out where to get medical equipment and supplies, which Chuck needed more as time went on.

Chuck lost his breath late one night. Louise called 911. As usual, the ambulance arrived within five minutes, and the paramedics strapped an oxygen mask to his face. However, by the time they got to the hospital, Chuck had a breathing tube down his windpipe, connected to a ventilator. He went straight to the intensive care unit (ICU). Although this happens commonly in advanced lung disease, no one had warned Chuck and Louise about it.

It took five days to wean Chuck off the ventilator. Even with oxygen blasting through a face mask, he could barely breathe on his own as he was wheeled out of the ICU. After a week and a half on the medical ward, his doctors decided he was too weak and confused to go home, so they arranged for placement in a nursing home.

Louise was shocked—but this was just the first of many rude awakenings. Medicare paid for a month of nursing home costs. However, as soon as it became clear that Chuck would never be well enough to come home, the bills started coming to Louise instead. The nursing home, she discovered, cost $65,000 a year. Medicaid would pay for most of it, but to qualify, she had to spend all their savings first.

The worst part for Louise was watching Chuck suffer. Constantly short of breath and in pain, confused, and weak, he was shuttled from nursing home to hospital and back. In the emergency department, they seemed to do the same tests every time. He howled in pain every time they stuck that big needle into his wrist to check his blood oxygen.

Every day Louise sat faithfully by Chuck's bedside. But at night she lay awake and worried. How would they manage now that their savings were gone?

One afternoon a hospital doctor burst through the door and said to Louise, "Sorry, there's nothing more we can do. We're referring your husband to hospice." Panicked and confused, she heard little else that was said by the doctor or by a parade of nurses, discharge planners, social workers, and others.

Finally, their message sank in: Chuck was dying. Therefore, he had to leave the hospital as soon as possible.

Louise couldn't understand. What was a hospital for? Plus, Chuck didn't look any different, except that he was sleepier than usual and his fingernails were blue. Louise was curious about this, but she was too shy to ask what it might mean.

The next morning, the ambulance took Chuck back to the nursing home. The hospice people met them there. For the first time since Louise could remember, his breathing seemed normal and he was finally comfortable. She went home to bed.

Late that night Louise's phone rang. It was the nursing home. Chuck was dead.

This is "usual care" in America. If some of the systems this chapter describes are in place, seriously ill people can get care on their own terms; otherwise, they will get treatment, usually in the hospital, until it no longer helps. A few will find comfort in hospice for their final days—or, as in Chuck's case, their final hours.

Usual Care of Advanced Illness

Why does our healthcare system so often fail those who need it most? Our sickest, weakest, and most vulnerable citizens undergo treatment that frequently does not improve their health. Beyond that, our system really isn't a system at all. Doctors and nurses don't talk to each other, patients lurch from one crisis to another, and families are forced to grope through this darkness alone to find solutions, if there are any. And the sicker the patient, the more chaotic the care becomes. Worst of all, the cost of this care is now rising so rapidly that, if nothing changes, the system itself may not survive.

Let's take a look at the population we're talking about and how we treat them.

Advanced illness occurs when one or more chronic diseases progress to the point where general health and functioning decline, response to treatment is reduced, and care needs increase, sometimes to the end of life. With advanced illness, visits to the emergency department increase. Prognosis and treatment plans become uncertain. Patients' personal goals and preferences may change. But too often, doctors and patients never talk about these things. So these patients continue to undergo intensive, expensive treatment that they don't really want. In America, this is usual care.

Usual care for advanced illness is responsible for a large and growing proportion of U.S. healthcare spending. Five percent of the population now accounts for 50% of our healthcare costs.[1] The majority of these expenditures are for treatment of advanced chronic illness. More than one-quarter of all Medicare expenditures are for treatment provided to patients in the last year of life. Then, as death approaches, hospital treatment and costs explode. Forty percent of this final year's spending occurs during the last *month* of life, 80% of it for hospital treatment.[2] It is hard to escape the conclusion that our healthcare system is waging an all-out war against death that is both fruitless and mindless.

The well-being of our elders, the sustainability of our healthcare system, and the viability of our economy are all threatened by this approach. An even greater threat, however, hangs over our families. Right now, as Louise discovered, almost one-third of American families with a seriously ill member, even those with health insurance, are forced to spend most or all of their life savings on care for their loved ones.[3]

The Origins of Usual Care

What we now call usual care developed during a time of great scientific progress. In the early 1900s, to exploit the new knowledge, medical treatment and training were concentrated in hospitals. By midcentury, this approach had vanquished some of the great scourges of human history. Bacterial infections, trauma, and complications of childbirth had all yielded to hospital treatment.

This was revolutionary. Never before had doctors had the power to *cure*. For the first time, we had mastered diseases that for millennia had struck down our loved ones without warning and reduced us to helpless bystanders.

Our success had a monumental impact on cultural attitudes and expectations about the nature of illness and about the potency of healthcare. Vast public resources were dedicated to the advancement of medical science. This campaign had impressive results. For example, death rates from coronary heart disease, the major killer of Western society, fell by more than 50% from 1950 to 1999.[4]

Then, gradually and without noticing, we became victims of our own success. The very patients who would have died suddenly from coronary disease survived to create a new epidemic of heart failure, now the most frequent cause of hospital admission and readmission in the United States.[5] We have traded acute disease for chronic illness, yet we cling stubbornly to outmoded treatments that were designed to react to acute events, not to solve chronic problems. We are just now beginning to confront this new reality.

Higher Costs, Diminishing Returns

At the turn of the twenty-first century, evidence is growing that our approach of "cure at all costs" is no longer working:

- Our half-century-long "war on cancer" has won few recent victories. Yes, cures have been found for some childhood malignancies. However, mortality rates remain high in the most common adult cancers, for

example, those of the lung and colon.[6] In noncancer disease, our record is
no better. For elderly people with heart failure, both hospitalization and
mortality rates have changed little over time despite new treatments.[7]

- A recent survey of the world literature on advanced noncancer disease
  reveals that for almost all diagnostic groups, (1) six-month survival,
  on average, is easy to predict, using common clinical factors, and (2)
  past this point, few if any treatments prolong life.[8] Yet patients in this
  closing phase undergo the most intensive treatment and accrue the
  highest costs.[2]

- Care for patients with advanced illness in the United States is fragmented, costly, and driven not by patients' personal choices but, rather, by
  hospital and physician supply, local practice patterns, and other system
  characteristics.[9] Reducing treatment costs to levels seen in the lowest-
  spending regions of the United States would not worsen and might
  improve patient outcomes, including mortality rates.[10] Instead, the volume and costs of hospital treatment for patients with advanced illness
  are rising over time.[11] These trends will worsen as our population ages.

- In advanced illness, comfort measures alone may keep patients alive as
  effectively as hospital treatment. Near the end of life, data show that
  hospice, commonly regarded as "merely" comfort care for the dying,
  may prolong life just as effectively as usual care. Compared with heart
  failure patients who undergo standard medical treatment, including
  hospitalization, those who enroll in hospice instead gain, on average,
  87 days of additional life, or about three months more than they gain
  with usual care.[12] The reasons for this are not yet clear. Reducing stress
  and pain may help to prolong life. Preventing exposure to hospital-
  based infections and medical errors may help, as well. Regardless of the
  cause, however, few people get to enjoy the survival benefits conveyed
  by hospice. As happened to Chuck, hospice referrals usually occur only
  after all treatment options have failed. Because of this, median survival
  across the United States after hospice enrollment today is fewer than

three weeks, and up to 15% of hospice patients die, as Chuck did, fewer than 24 hours after enrollment.[13]

The bottom line is that usual care does not produce the same benefits in chronic illness that it did when acute events dominated the clinical scene. Simply providing more usual care does not extend lives or improve quality of life. In fact, it harms patients. Beyond that, it threatens the sustainability of Medicare.

Public perceptions and beliefs have not yet caught up with this new evidence. Many Americans continue to believe that more care is better regardless of its cost. In a recent nationwide poll, 55% agreed that "the healthcare system in this country has the medical technology and the expertise to offer treatments to seriously ill patients and should spend whatever it takes to extend their lives."[14]

More and more people like Chuck and Louise are finding that this investment isn't paying off. But another kind of investment, in new programs that provide care that people really want and need in their homes and communities, can provide a much bigger payoff.

Advanced Illness Management 1.0: Advance Care Planning Where People Live

In 1998, Sutter Care at Home (then Sutter VNA and Hospice) received a grant from the Robert Wood Johnson Foundation to develop a home-based intervention using a nurse practitioner and social worker for people with advanced illness.[15] The intervention was designed for Medicare health maintenance organizations (HMOs), but when reimbursement decreased, most of these organizations didn't survive. As they closed, we were told to stop our project.

Instead, we redesigned our model to operate within home health. To avoid the association with dying that had plagued hospice and palliative care, we named the new program Advanced Illness Management, or AIM.

In 2003, AIM 1.0 was first implemented in our largest home health branch. We taught nurses and social workers to help patients and families with advance care planning and to provide information about hospice, and we also emphasized pain and symptom management. Regular team meetings focused on case-based teaching. In 2006 we published a paper showing significant increases in hospice enrollment rates, particularly among local African American residents,[16] who as a group tend to underutilize hospice care.

By 2007, AIM had attracted increasing attention both within and outside Sutter Health. Doctors told us they found it easier, clinically and emotionally, to identify and enroll an "AIM patient" than it was to refer patients to hospice. AIM spread to all nine of our agency branches within Sutter. Other grantors came forward to offer additional support. Today, more than 7,000 people have enrolled in AIM 1.0 throughout northern California.

AIM 2.0: Multidimensional Care Management

In late 2009, an upgraded version of AIM for home-health-eligible patients was piloted at two Sacramento hospitals with two physician groups. In March 2010, "AIM 2.0" was opened to all patients with advanced illness regardless of home health eligibility, and in October the program spread to all physician groups and hospitals affiliated with Sutter Health and served by Sutter Care at Home in Sacramento and the Sierra foothills.

AIM 2.0 objectives included reduced emergency and hospital use, reduced physician burden, more robust palliative outcomes, and increased patient/family/caregiver engagement. An overarching goal was to move the primary site of care out of the hospital and into the patient's place of residence. Likewise, the focus of care changed, from reacting to acute events to responding to the ill person's personal goals, preventing crises, and coordinating care across all settings and over time to the end of life. Instead of patients being made to come to providers, multidisciplinary teams brought care to seriously ill people in their homes and facilities.

In the hospital, inpatient AIM Care Coordinators (ACCs) interfaced with hospitalists, inpatient palliative care consultation teams, emergency department staff, case managers, and discharge planners. The ACCs assessed patients for risk of readmission and enrolled high-risk patients in AIM. Concurrently, they implemented transition protocols to prepare patients and their families for discharge and started the educational and planning program that would be continued when patients returned home.

AIM Care Managers were also embedded in physician group practices, where they could consult with doctors and other clinicians about individual patients and also provide telephone management.

At the same time, AIM 2.0 care processes in the home were standardized, including assessment and self-management of "red flag" symptoms that could signal the need for hospitalization; assessment and treatment of depression; medication reconciliation and management; coordinating follow-up visits; and advance care planning, including completion of Physician Orders for Life-Sustaining Treatment (POLST) forms, by now a legal standard in California. Personal health records were also instituted.

Reduced Utilization and Costs

In early 2011, pilot results were evaluated for the first 240 patients enrolled in AIM 2.0 between November 2009 and November 2010. Average age was 76 years. About one-third had cancer and another third heart failure; 54% had more than one condition. More than one-third were referred from physician practices, and a similar proportion came from hospitals. Almost three-fourths of patients were covered by Medicare; about 60% of these were Medicare fee-for-service.

Advance care planning was effective. Ninety-six percent of all AIM 2.0 enrollees had POLST forms signed. One hundred percent had implemented crisis plans. About two-thirds had enrolled in hospice. Both hospital days and physicians' visits per decedent in the last six months of life were reduced to levels reported for the best performers in the Dartmouth Atlas.[17]

Utilization and costs were reduced, particularly in the hospital. AIM enrollees were hospitalized less and for shorter periods. This was significant because (1) patients with advanced illness under usual care tend to undergo more and longer hospitalizations as illness progresses and (2) the Sutter Sacramento area was already a benchmark performer in the Dartmouth Atlas prior to AIM 2.0 implementation.[9] Finally, this analysis was performed on pilot data; performance may be expected to increase with experience.

All utilization and costs were measured at 30, 60, and 90 days both pre- and post-AIM enrollment, so each enrollee served as his or her own control. Patients who died or who were discharged to hospice were excluded from the analysis; when they were included, the results presented below were even better.

On the inpatient side, at 90 days after enrollment compared with the 90 days before, AIM enrollees experienced a 58% reduction in hospital admissions, a 63% reduction in ICU days, and a 21% reduction in hospital length of stay (LOS) on subsequent admissions. This amounted to a two-day reduction in LOS per admission, which resulted in substantial hospital savings. On the downside, preventing hospital admissions reduced hospital revenue. However, total direct inpatient care costs were cut by a larger margin. On the bottom line, hospitals enjoyed a positive net contribution margin of $1,333 per AIM enrollment.

This is important to emphasize because many hospital administrators object to care management interventions designed to reduce admissions and readmissions out of a fear of a potential negative impact on their bottom line. On the contrary, our data show that reducing "heads in beds" can result in net savings at the hospital level.

For physician groups, visits by AIM enrollees at 90 days were reduced by 46%. This benefitted the groups, which lose money on Medicare patient visits and anticipate higher losses from Medicare reimbursement cuts in the future. On the other hand, physician telephone encounters increased by 10% over the same period. Thus, physician productivity was improved, and at the same time the physician-patient relationship was preserved. Reducing visits in this population also benefits patients, since many are homebound or travel to physician appointments only with difficulty. Even if they make the trip, their encounters tend to be long and complex. Not surprisingly, physicians reported high levels of satisfaction with AIM's home-based approach and saw AIM clinicians as an integral part of their team.

Finally, enrollment increases of 60% were noted in hospice and 49% in home health. This did not offset the costs to Sutter Care at Home of implementing the program. However, when patient care costs alone were evaluated, the healthcare system as a whole broke even. Hospitals, doctors, and home-based services together saved about $90 per month for each person enrolled in AIM. However, payers, especially Medicare, saved about $1,250 per enrollee per month, or $15,000 per enrollee per year.

Estimating national savings from these data is challenging. However, if an advanced care intervention like AIM were provided to the 5% of the U.S. population that currently accrues 50% of all healthcare costs, and if only 10% of these savings were realized, the total would amount to about $25 billion. This alone wouldn't balance Medicare's budget, but it could easily help finance a nationwide system of advanced care that overcomes important shortcomings of our current system.

Three Dimensions of Health System Fragmentation

Care of people with advanced illness in the United States is fragmented along three distinct but related dimensions: space, time, and treatment. The first dimension of fragmentation, the spatial or geographic, has been widely debated in healthcare reform because dysfunctional or nonexistent relationships among providers scattered among various treatment settings are so obviously responsible for problems at all stages of illness. The other two dimensions have not received as much attention. However, they impact care to an increasing degree as illness becomes advanced.

These three dimensions of health system fragmentation may be described as follows:

1. **Space.** Patient transitions between healthcare settings are sometimes poorly managed.[18] Prescriptions may be lost and physician appointments missed. Thousands of dollars' worth of clinical progress from days of hospital treatment may be wasted within 24 hours of discharge from hospital to home. Other sites and sources of care are also poorly connected. Hospitalists are often cut off from primary care physicians. Communication among primary and specialty physicians may be spotty. Home care and community agencies can be the last to know when their patients call 911 and return to the hospital. In short, our system is broken.

2. **Time.** Acute illness, the kind that usual care was designed for, occurs in brief episodes. Either patients recover or they don't. But chronic illness progresses over time, and treatment must evolve as illness progresses. Early forms of diabetes, for example, are treated with diet and oral medication, but later forms may require insulin injections. Ideally, treatment is standardized according to the best available evidence. Deviation from these standards may be regarded as medical negligence. However, as chronic disease progresses to advanced illness, treatment is no longer dictated simply by objective community standards of practice. As burdens of treatment come to outweigh benefits, patient goals and preferences for care may be driven increasingly by considerations related to quality of life rather than quantity. But if personal goals are not discussed and clinicians' goals stay the same, treatment continues reflexively. Patients may undergo unwanted hospitalizations, tests, and procedures. This is overtreatment, or medical waste. It does not contribute to positive outcomes, and it needlessly increases costs.

3. **Treatment.** Acute care medicine's success has blinded us to the inexorable progression of chronic illness. Curative measures are applied until

they no longer work. At that point clinicians may say, as they did to Louise, that nothing more can be done. This is clearly not true. Palliative care has shown that there is plenty to do even when a cure is no longer possible. Unfortunately, reimbursement and regulations, particularly the Medicare hospice benefit, have taught clinicians to categorize patients as either "treatable" or "dying." Patient care has been fractured into two mutually exclusive segments: "curative care" and "comfort care." This is an artificial distinction that makes truly continuous care impossible to provide.

Fragmentation along dimensions of **space, time,** and **treatment** leads to loss of data, duplication of tests, failure of advance directives, unhelpful and unwanted hospitalizations, and burgeoning costs. Worse, this fragmentation fosters uncertainty and fear as patients and families are forced to find their own way through our dysfunctional system when they are already stressed by the physical, emotional, and financial burdens of chronic illness.

Healing the System: Care Management in Three Dimensions

Research shows that care of a defined group of high-cost Medicare beneficiaries with multiple chronic illnesses can be significantly improved through care management.[19] Each of these three "degrees of separation" can be mended through care management specific to that dimension. Quality of care may be increased and costs reduced in proportion to how many of these dimensions of fragmentation are addressed and how effectively usual discontinuities of care are bridged in each dimension.

Innovative interventions in advanced care address all three of these dimensions of fragmentation. Research and policy change are needed to make these interventions scalable and sustainable. Care management is not currently reimbursed by most payers, particularly Medicare. Yet Medicare savings achieved by advanced care programs would be more than enough to finance their implementation nationwide.

Care management that heals fragmentation in these three dimensions may be described as follows:

1. **Space.** Care management across the spatial or geographic dimension can be achieved through system integration among hospitals, physician groups, home- and community-based care, and long-term care. This connectivity across treatment settings is a core element of delivery system reform intended to promote more seamless and transparent care. Accountable care organizations (ACOs), bundled payments, and other models are intended to encourage provider groups to integrate their care in this way. Implementing advanced care directly promotes this kind of system integration.

2. **Time.** Integrating care across the time dimension is accomplished through advance care planning. Starting this process as early as possible, say, with a first discussion at age 55, then with further programmed conversations at diagnosis of life-limiting illness, and again when illness becomes advanced, can help patients make decisions that truly reflect their personal preferences.[20] Documenting these decisions and making them available at every potential point of care then depend on effective execution of the first, or spatial, dimension of care management.

3. **Treatment.** Before scientific medicine became the dominant paradigm, most clinical interventions for advanced illnesses were palliative—that is, oriented toward comfort rather than cure. But modern medicine swung the pendulum to the opposite extreme, where cure became the ideal until it was no longer achievable. For patients with advanced illness, a newer care continuum is necessary, employing an integrated approach that discards outmoded distinctions between "active treatment" and "comfort care." Advanced care employs a customized mix of disease-modifying

treatment and palliative care that evolves with illness progression and tracks closely individual and personal preferences and goals.

Person-Centered Care over Patient-Centered Care

"Patient-centered care" has become a mantra for healthcare reformers. Of course healthcare should provide a better experience for patients. But patient-centered care is actually a provider-centric term. It assumes that *people* have already become *patients*. **Person-centered care,** on the other hand, brings people with advanced illness only the care they want, where and when they want it. Many seriously ill people feel that quality of life is more important than length of life.[21] In other words, they would prefer not to be patients.

Most people with advanced illness prefer to remain in their homes, independent and comfortable, for as long as possible. They prefer to avoid hospitalization because it is disruptive and uncomfortable. For the seriously ill, even traveling to the doctor's office can be an ordeal.

Usual care is based on crisis management. Keeping seriously ill people independent at home is not its goal. Care management, on the other hand, anticipates and prevents crises through enhanced home-based interventions.

To keep people from becoming patients, innovative programs focus on the immediate, personal goals of the person who is ill. Personal goals are not necessarily clinical. When asked what he or she really wants, a person with advanced illness might say, "I just want to be able to walk to the dinner table to eat with my family."

A clinician trained in usual care might find this an intriguing but irrelevant aspect of the social history. Innovative care management programs, on the other hand, tailor their plans specifically to these personal goals and then use motivational interviewing and other specialized techniques to "get on the same side of the table" with the ill person in order to manage medications, note and report symptoms, or stay in close touch with primary doctors.

This person-centered approach improves care and reduces costs because

- People become more motivated for self-management when they are trying to get what they most want rather than trying to "do what the doctor says" and
- Moving the focus of care from hospital to home and community increases satisfaction with care, adherence to medical plans, and contact with primary care providers. Preventing one day of hospitalization pays for many days of care at home and in the community.

Cost Control Is Important, but It's Not the Point

Because Medicare's future is in doubt if healthcare spending is not controlled, innovative clinical ideas will not be sustainable on the national level unless they produce cost savings. However, the idea of lowering costs by reducing services for seriously ill patients has been a nonstarter. Even suggesting a small payment to physicians for holding advance care planning conversations with their patients brought forth a storm of "death panel" rhetoric.[22]

Advanced care, however, is not designed to save money. It is designed to get seriously ill people the care they want and need. It does not "balance the budget on the backs of sick people." Cost savings are an unintended side benefit of person-centered care management.

Person-centered care avoids the fundamental mistake that brought down managed care: it does not attempt to prevent unnecessary treatment. No one can know in advance what procedure, hospitalization, or ICU stay might be unnecessary. Managed care hired "gatekeepers" to do this, but the strategy backfired. Gatekeepers are agents of providers, payers, or both. Their job, by definition, is to ration care. Managed care failed because it really managed finances instead of care.[23]

Advanced care, on the other hand, does not try to decide what care is unnecessary. Its job is to prevent only treatment that is **unwanted**. At all times, it gives people free choice about their care. With enough education over repeated sessions at home about disease process, potential outcomes, and all available care options, competent ill persons can decide what they do and don't want. They can plan at their own pace rather than in the heat of battle after a crisis has occurred. Preventing unwanted tests, treatments, and hospitalizations this way is not controversial.

Of course, a small number of seriously ill people and their families will always want everything done, even when they know all the alternatives. However, data from model advanced care programs show that the vast majority of enrollees don't want intensive hospital treatment once they learn, often from direct experience, that advanced care can prevent the crisis-driven lifestyle dictated by usual care.

Advanced Care in Action

At age 27, Jenny F. had already lived longer than many people with cystic fibrosis (CF), an incurable genetic disease that clogs the lungs with sticky secretions that eventually make it impossible to breathe. As CF becomes advanced, its victims get pneumonia and spend longer and longer periods in the hospital on intravenous (IV) antibiotics. Over the past few years, Jenny had suffered through many hospitalizations, two lung transplants, chronic pain, shortness of breath, and the ravages of drug abuse. She lived in a tiny inner-city apartment with her father, Ray, and her seven-year-old daughter, Stacy.

Jenny had a simple plan. It had three parts: (1) to live as long as possible for the sake of her daughter, (2) to keep going to the emergency department, and (3) to die in the hospital on a ventilator so Stacy wouldn't have to see her suffer. Ray, who was in complete agreement with Jenny, would decide when to tell the doctors to turn off the ventilator and let her go.

Jenny liked the hospital. She felt secure there, she sometimes breathed better, and, best of all, she got a short vacation. Above all, she was a young mother with a raging desire to survive.

After Jenny came onto AIM, she was hospitalized three more times in three months. Then she let the AIM team bring IV antibiotics to her home and treat her there. Over the next four months, she got weaker and more breathless, but she didn't go back to the hospital. She came to trust her AIM nurse and finally accepted oral morphine. This helped her pain and breathing trouble, and to her surprise, it didn't make her the least bit drowsy. She signed a do-not-resuscitate (DNR) order, but she still wanted to go back to the hospital because she was "afraid of drowning" at the end of life. She didn't even want to hear about hospice.

After another two months, however, Jenny decided she didn't need to go back to the hospital after all. She tried one more course of IV antibiotics at home, but it didn't help her feel any better. Finally, she agreed to talk to a hospice nurse. She decided hospice wasn't a bad idea after all and signed on.

This is a common scenario among people with advanced illness. For them, if they get the right kind of support, "the body is the teacher." They learn how their bodies change with illness, and they learn to adjust to it. They make plans and often change them as their illness progresses. Many learn to work with their illness, rather than fighting it every step of the way. Many actually live longer this way than they would if they stayed in the battle zone of usual care.

Jenny lived another six weeks, comfortable and secure at home. She, Stacy, and Ray all adjusted over time to the reality of her illness and, finally, to the reality of her death. When it came to Jenny, it happened quietly at home, with Stacy and Ray by her side. It was something they never thought they'd have the strength to do when Jenny was healthier, but by the time she died, they'd forgotten that. It just seemed natural.

Advanced Care: A National Model Is Needed

Stories like this would be commonplace if a national pilot of advanced care were implemented by the Centers for Medicare and Medicaid Innovation (CMMI). The programs described in this book all employ evidence-based care management methods that have already been scientifically proven and used to construct programs that have had success locally and regionally.[24-26]

The next step is to meld the best practices from these programs into a unified clinical model and to test it nationwide. A national pilot of advanced care would

- Implement a multisite study, with sites in most or all Medicare regions;
- Standardize metrics across all sites to compare results and to define best practices;
- Employ evaluation that does not use rigid randomized clinical trial methodology but, rather, an iterative "learn-as-you-go" strategy that results in reliable and reproducible process and outcome improvement among sites;
- Modify misaligned payment structures to support better care by adjusting current payment streams to support advanced care management and then by evolving into a geographically risk-adjusted global payment system with a shared savings arrangement; and
- Demonstrate cost-effectiveness to the Centers for Medicare and Medicaid Services by showing that advanced care achieves simultaneous improvements in both quality and cost.

Previous trials of advanced care in single locations have allowed skeptics to ascribe positive results to unique characteristics of those communities rather than to the advanced care intervention itself. A national pilot would transcend that barrier. It would also disseminate more widely a useful attribute of advanced care: **system integration**. Advanced care implementation promotes integration of hospitals, physician groups, and home- and community-based services. This would heal the first dimension of system fragmentation, the spatial or geographic dimension, and help providers prepare for future shared-risk reimbursement models.

Finally, implementing a national model of advanced care would deal with a nagging problem of delivery system reform: how to change medical culture.

Doctors and nurses don't change the way they treat their patients because of theoretical models, white papers, and lectures. Only one thing changes the way clinicians think and act: changing the structure of the system in which they practice. Implementing advanced care changes not only care processes and patient outcomes but also attitudes and practices. Just as advanced care helps seriously ill people change how they think, feel, and make decisions, it helps clinicians do the same.

To Heal the Patient, Heal the System

Healthcare in the United States is the most technically advanced in the world, yet every day we abandon some of our most vulnerable citizens, those grappling with the physical, emotional, and financial challenges of advanced illness. We abandon them not through neglect but to treatment by a fragmented system afflicted by inefficiency and rising costs.

We can prevent our system from failing those who need it the most by ensuring that they get the care they want and the freedom they deserve. Advanced care can help them to heal even when a cure isn't possible. It can also help to heal our healthcare.

Dr. Brad Stuart is a general internist who attended Stanford University School of Medicine. He is currently chief medical officer of Sutter Care at Home, the largest home care and hospice provider in northern California. He founded the Advanced Illness Management (AIM) program, which integrates hospitals, medical groups, and home- and community-based services to improve care and reduce costs for patients with late-stage chronic illness. Dr. Stuart was the primary author in 1996 of *Medical Guidelines for Prognosis in Selected Non-Cancer Diseases*, adopted as national Medicare hospice eligibility criteria. He has received the Heart of Hospice Award from the National Hospice and Palliative Care Organization, as well as the California State Hospice Association's Pierre Salmon Award. In 2007 he was voted "Physician of the Year" by the California Association for Health Services at Home. He is a founding board member of the Coalition to Transform Advanced Care (C-TAC), a Washington, DC–based initiative dedicated to national delivery system redesign, policy development, public engagement, and professional education to measurably improve care for people with advanced illness. Dr. Stuart was featured in the HBO documentary *Letting Go: A Hospice Journey* and wrote and hosted *Care beyond Cure: Hospice Helping Physicians Treat the Terminally Ill*, a nationally televised special that won an International Angel Award for Media Excellence. He has published widely and lectured internationally on medical, psychosocial, and spiritual issues at the end of life.

References

1. Zuvekas SH, Cohen JW. Prescription drugs and the changing concentration of health care expenditures. *Health Affairs (Millwood)*. 2007;26(1):249-257.

2. Eppig F. Last year of life expenditures. *MCBS Profiles*. 2003(10). https://www.cms.gov/mcbs/downloads/issue10.pdf. Accessed September 2, 2011.

3. The SUPPORT Investigators. A controlled trial to improve care for seriously ill hospitalized patients: the study to understand prognoses and preferences for outcomes and risks of treatments (SUPPORT). *JAMA: Journal of the American Medical Association*. 1995;274(20):22-29.

4. Fox CS, Evans JC, Larson MG, Kannel WB, Levy D. Temporal trends in coronary heart disease mortality and sudden cardiac death from 1950 to 1999: the Framingham Heart Study. *Circulation*. 2004;110(5):522-527.

5. Roger VL, Weston SA, Redfield MM, et al. Trends in heart failure incidence and survival in a community-based population. *JAMA: Journal of the American Medical Association*. 2004;292(3):344-350.

6. Leaf C. Why we're losing the war on cancer (and how to win it). *Fortune*. 2004;149(6):76-82, 84-86, 88 passim.

7.   Curtis LH, Greiner MA, Hammill BG, et al. Early and long-term outcomes of heart failure in elderly persons, 2001–2005. *Archives of Internal Medicine.* 2008;168(22):2481-2488.

8.   Salpeter SR, Luo EJ, Malter DS, Stuart B. Systematic review of non-cancer presentations with a median survival of 6 months or less [published online ahead of print October 25 2011] *American Journal of Medicine.* 2011. http://www.sciencedirect.com/science/article/pii/S0002934311006462. Accessed November 3, 2011.

9.   Wennberg JE, Fisher ES, Goodman DC, Skinner JS. Tracking the care of patients with severe chronic illness. *Dartmouth Atlas of Health Care 2008.* http://www.dartmouthatlas.org/downloads/atlases/2008_Chronic_Care_Atlas.pdf. Accessed September 2, 2011.

10. Fisher ES, Wennberg DE, Stukel TA, Gottlieb DJ, Lucas FL, Pinder EL. The implications of regional variations in Medicare spending. Pt. 2. Health outcomes and satisfaction with care. *Annals of Internal Medicine.* 2003;138(4):288-298.

11. Goodman DC, Esty AR, Fisher ES, Chang C. Trends and variations in end-of-life care for Medicare beneficiaries with severe chronic illness. http://www.rwjf.org/qualityequality/product.jsp?id=72192. Accessed September 2, 2011.

12. Connor SR, Pyenson B, Fitch K, Spence C, Iwasaki K. Comparing hospice and nonhospice patient survival among patients who die within a three-year window. *Journal of Pain and Symptom Management.* 2007;33(3):238-246.

13. NHPCO facts and figures: hospice care in America. 2010. http://www.nhpco.org/files/public/Statistics_Research/Hospice_Facts_Figures_Oct-2010.pdf. Accessed October 19, 2011.

14. Living well at the end of life: a national conversation. *National Journal* Web site. http://syndication.nationaljournal.com/communications/NationalJournalRegenceToplines.pdf. Updated 2011. Accessed September 2, 2011.

15. Stuart B, D'Onofrio CN, Boatman S, Feigelman G. CHOICES: promoting early access to end-of-life care through home-based transition management. *Journal of Palliative Medicine.* 2003;6(4):671-683.

16. Ciemins EL, Stuart B, Gerber R, Newman J, Bauman M. An evaluation of the advanced illness management (AIM) program: increasing hospice utilization in the San Francisco Bay area. *Journal of Palliative Medicine.* 2006;9(6):1401-1411.

17. Data comparing hospital performance in these domains may be found at http://www.dartmouthatlas.org/data/hospital/.

18. Naylor MD, Brooten D, Campbell R, et al. Comprehensive discharge planning and home follow-up of hospitalized elders: a randomized clinical trial. *JAMA: Journal of the American Medical Association*. 1999;281(7):613-620.

19. Bodenheimer T, Berry-Millett R. Care management of patients with complex health care needs. Research synthesis report no. 19, 2009. http://www.rwjf.org/files/research/52372caremgt.rpt.revised.pdf. Accessed September 2, 2011.

20. Hammes BJ. Personal communication.

21. Barnato AE, Herndon MB, Anthony DL, et al. Are regional variations in end-of-life care intensity explained by patient preferences? A study of the US Medicare population. *Medical Care*. 2007;45(5):386-393.

22. Pear R. Obama returns to end-of-life plan that caused stir. *New York Times*. December 25, 2010. http://www.nytimes.com/2010/12/26/us/politics/26death.html. Accessed September 2, 2011.

23. Robinson JC. The end of managed care. *JAMA: Journal of the American Medical Association*. 2001;285(20):2622-2628.

24. Meyer H. Changing the conversation in California about care near the end of life. *Health Affairs (Millwood)*. 2011;30(3):390-393.

25. Krakauer R, Spettell CM, Reisman L, Wade MJ. Opportunities to improve the quality of care for advanced illness. *Health Affairs (Millwood)*. 2009;28(5):1357-1359.

26. Hammes BJ, Rooney BL, Gundrum JD. A comparative, retrospective, observational study of the prevalence, availability, and specificity of advance care plans in a county that implemented an advance care planning microsystem. *Journal of the American Geriatrics Society*. 2010;58(7):1249-1255.

nine

Impact of Health Plan Management of Advanced Illness: The Aetna Compassionate Care Program

—Randall Krakauer, MD, MBA,
and Wayne Rawlins, MD, MBA

IN 2003, A group of clinical leaders at Aetna reviewed current practices and new opportunities in the way "End-of-Life Care" (the terminology we used at the time) was provided. The ACOVE[1] study had recently reviewed quality of care for the elderly and determined that the quality was disappointing for the treatment of many medical conditions and that the quality of care ranking for end-of-life care was at the bottom. Indeed, if one evaluates the core components of care at this stage—discussion of choices and options early in the course of an advanced illness, psychosocial support, pain relief, and palliative care—our healthcare system was doing a poor job for people with advanced illness.

"Today, our healthcare system is failing to meet the needs of the dying, which can include pain and symptom management, help in achieving a sense of control, and support for the emotional and spiritual needs of both patients and their caregivers," said John W. Rowe, MD, Aetna chairman and CEO at the time. To address this critical issue in healthcare, Aetna developed a program to meet the needs of its members with end-of-life care needs. Using evidence-based literature and the advice of nationally known experts, Aetna implemented the Aetna Compassionate Care Program. Aetna's Compassionate Care Program allows members facing the advanced stages of an illness to continue receiving the medical treatment that they and their physicians believe is important while enabling them to achieve the commonly voiced objective of dying with dignity, in a place where they are comfortable, with those whom they love most. We believe it is important for these members to know their options and feel empowered to make meaningful decisions in concert with their family and physicians. Our goal is to give our members choices and autonomy in the care they receive at one of the most critical times of their lives, the final years and months.

While the cost of care provided in the final year in Medicare beneficiaries' lives was estimated to be approximately 30% of total Medicare cost,[2] much of this care seemed ineffective. The SUPPORT trial had recently been completed, and this intervention had yielded disappointing results.[3] In response, we set out to devise an exemplary program that would have a real impact on what we felt was an extraordinary opportunity at the intersection of quality and cost. We had developed a robust case management capability, particularly for Medicare, and were determined to deploy these skills and improve end-of-life care for our members.

There were three primary components to implementation of the Compassionate Care Program, including:

- Training and mentoring our nurse case managers in palliative care, including quality, engagement, and cultural issues; an ability to identify members in need of such service; and making appropriate outreach to such members. Our nurse case managers interact with our members and family caregivers principally over the telephone, which sometimes presents certain challenges in terms of engagement. However, in our experience we have found that our nurse case managers are regularly able to get very close to the members through a telephonic relationship, often receiving sensitive information from members who might have difficulty sharing the same information in a face-to-face setting.

- Enhanced benefits for commercial members (not possible for Medicare Advantage, given Medicare rules). This involved eliminating the requirement that members stop curative therapy in order to become eligible for hospice benefits. We also changed the requirement that a member be certified by a physician as terminal from 6 months to 12 months.

- User-friendly, culturally sensitive, and easily accessible Web-based decision support tools and information for consumers regarding palliative care and end-of-life care.

When designing the Compassionate Care Program, we added expert support to members in the form of trained nurse case managers. We felt that discussions of choices and care plans for members with advanced illness were begun too late or not at all, thus depriving members and families of the option of informed choices. On the basis of the experience of the SUPPORT group[3] in providing the results of such discussions to physicians, we elected to have our case managers—after consulting with physicians and their office staffs—initiate discussions with members and families.

To facilitate the effectiveness of the program, we elected to remove what we thought were artificial barriers to member choice. For example, we believe that the requirement that a member stop curative therapy to be eligible for hospice benefits serves no useful purpose. If the idea of a patient in hospice receiving curative therapy seems a contradiction, perhaps the best way to resolve it is with the hospice. Acceptance of one's mortality is a process, not an epiphany. This barrier requires that the patient and family go through this difficult process, perhaps without any support, in order to receive such support.

We expected that case management and benefit liberalization would improve care for members with terminal illness. We decided to test our plan with three groups: (1) commercial (non-Medicare) insured who would receive the specialized case management, (2) commercial members who would receive the case management and also the hospice benefit liberalization, and (3) Medicare Advantage members who would receive the case management (on the basis of the terms of their Medicare Advantage plan, which did not permit Aetna to liberalize the hospice benefit). For each of these groups, a recent matched historic control was created. Over the following year we were able to demonstrate dramatic impact for all groups.[4]

For the commercial case management group, hospice election went from 31% to 72%, while use of hospital days was reduced by 37%.[4] The hospice benefit liberalization commercial group experienced similar impact. Importantly, we liberalized the hospice benefit without increasing cost compared with the group with case management alone. Even for the Medicare Advantage group (which did not have the benefit liberalization), we showed an increased hospice election rate, an 82% decrease in acute days, an 88% decrease in intensive care days, and an 82% decrease in emergency room utilization. In all cases, member and family satisfaction was high.[5] In fact, despite several years of experience, we have not received a single member complaint on this program, which is significant, considering the number of participants and the sensitive nature of the issues that are often discussed. Table 1 shows our results against control groups for the three groups studied.

The impact associated with telephonic case management was dramatic and represents an extant target for any such program. One might expect results at least this impressive with management by primary care physicians or palliative care specialists. In our opinion, the demonstration that this is possible through telephone contact, which can be provided nearly everywhere, creates an imperative that such services be made available universally to people with advanced illness. Though some provider organizations have reported comparable impact, to our knowledge this is the only demonstration of such effect on people with advanced illness by a health plan and with a process that has the potential of reaching large numbers of patients at a cost that would make provision of services

TABLE 1. The Effect of Case Management

	Enhanced Benefits Group		Commercial CM Group		Medicare CM Group	
	Study	Control	Study	Control	Study	Control
N	387	387	3,491	3,491	447	447
Average number of days in CM program	42.3	00	39.6	—	56.7	—
Percentage using hospice/respite	69.8	27.9	71.7	30.8	62.9	N/A
Mean days between first hospice claim and death	36.7	21.4	28.6	15.9	N/A	N/A
Hospice inpatient days/1,000 members	1,819	744	2,027	654	N/A	N/A
Hospice outpatient days/1,000 members	16,501	4,090	13,297	3,753	N/A	N/A
Percentage of members with acute inpatient stay	16.8	40.3	22.7	42.9	30.0	88.4
Average length of acute inpatient stay, days	6.19	7.06	6.54	5.97	7.28	8.26
Percentage of members with emergency visit	9.8	15.2	9.7	14.4	8.5	32.9
Percentage of members with ICU stay	9.6	23.0	11.7	19.9	14.8	50.6
Acute inpatient days/1,000 members	1,504	4,106	2,438	3,882	3,389	19,148
Emergency visits/1,000 members	96	230	137	197	107	474

highly feasible. This is applicable to anyone who can be reached by telephone, though potential for impact might vary due to other factors.

There may be no better opportunity at the intersection of quality and cost than management of advanced illness. Current practices represent not just large-scale misapplication of scarce healthcare resources but also a violation of informed patient choice, as many individuals make different choices when support and information for planning are provided.[6]

Since our study was completed, Aetna has made specialized Compassionate Care case management available to all medical members eligible for case management and has made benefit liberalization the standard for commercially insured medical members. As case managers have gained experience in this area, impact has continued to improve. For 2010, the hospice election rate for Medicare Advantage members in the program was 82%. We have also proposed to the Centers for Medicare and Medicaid Services that it allow Aetna to similarly liberalize the Medicare Advantage hospice benefit, at our financial risk.

A final note is important to understanding what has been achieved. The outcomes of Aetna's Compassionate Care Program are compelling, but they tell only part of the story. The most important part of the story is how this new approach to care touches people. This impact is achieved primarily through trained, experienced, and skilled case managers. This is more difficult to quantify, but the following case manager note captures what we see on an everyday basis.

"Wife stated member passed away with hospice. Much emotional support given to spouse. She talked about what a wonderful life they had together, their children, all of the people's lives that he touched. They were married 49 years last Thursday, and each year he would give her a piece of jewelry. On Tuesday when she walked into his room, he had a gift and card lying on his chest, a beautiful ring that he had their daughter purchase. She was happy he gave it to her on Tuesday—on Thursday he was not alert. She stated through his business he touched many people's lives, and they all

somehow knew he was sick, and he has received many flowers, meals, fruit, cakes. She stated her lawn had become overgrown, and the landscaper came and cleaned up the entire property, planted over 50 mums, placed cornstalks and pumpkins all around. She said she is so grateful for the outpouring of love. Also stated that hospice was wonderful, as well as everyone at the doctor's office, and everyone here at Aetna. . . . Encouraged her to call CM [case manager] with any issues or concerns. Closed to case mgmt."

This note reveals the close relationship that has developed between the case manager and the member's wife. It is this relationship that facilitates—indeed, enables—such impact. The success of the Compassionate Care Program is based primarily on the efforts of a cadre of dedicated and experienced case managers. Building this resource is what requires time, effort, and other resources. Our experience is that it is well worth the effort. There is perhaps no greater opportunity in medicine to influence the intersection of quality and cost.[7]

∽

Randall Krakauer, MD, MBA, graduated from Albany Medical College in 1972 and is board certified in internal medicine and rheumatology. He received training in internal medicine at the University of Minnesota Hospitals and in rheumatology at the National Institutes of Health and Massachusetts General Hospital/Harvard Medical School, and he received an MBA from Rutgers. He is a fellow of the American College of Physicians and the American College of Rheumatology and professor of medicine at Seton Hall University Graduate School of Medicine. He is past chairman of the American College of Managed Care Medicine.

Dr. Krakauer has more than 30 years of experience in medicine and medical management and has held senior medical management positions in several major organizations. He is responsible for medical management planning and implementation nationally for Aetna Medicare members, including program development and administration.

Wayne Rawlins, MD, MBA, is a national medical director for Racial and Ethnic Equality Initiatives at Aetna, reporting to Aetna's chief medical officer. In this role, Dr. Rawlins serves as the lead clinician focused on identifying activities to address racial and ethnic disparities in healthcare for Aetna's 18 million members. In 2009, he was appointed to the Institute of Medicine's Subcommittee on Standardized Collection of Race/Ethnicity Data for Healthcare Quality Improvement. Dr. Rawlins also serves as a member of National Quality Forum's Cultural Competency Expert Panel and is a member of the Regional Health Equity Council (Office of Minority Health) for Region 1.

While at Aetna, Dr. Rawlins served in several senior clinical operational roles prior to assuming his current role, including vice president of medical management for Aetna Government Health Plans, regional medical director for Aetna's northeast region, and head of business planning and reporting for National Medical Services. Dr. Rawlins also led the design, development, and implementation of the Aetna Compassionate Care Program, Aetna's industry-leading end-of-life care program.

Dr. Rawlins received his medical degree from the University of Connecticut and then completed an internal medicine residency and chief residency at the University of Rochester in New York. He is board certified in internal medicine. Dr. Rawlins received his MBA from Rensselaer Polytechnic Institute in 2001. Prior to joining Aetna, he was a physician manager with the Northeast Permanente Medical Group and treated a wide variety of patients in a busy primary care practice.

He is a member of the National Medical Association, the American College of Physicians, and the American College of Physician Executives.

References

1. Wenger NS, Shekelle PG. Assessing care of vulnerable elders: ACOVE project overview. *Annals of Internal Medicine*. 2001;135(8 Pt 2):642-646.

2. Hogan C, for the Medicare Payment Advisory Commission. Medicare beneficiaries' costs and use of care in the last year of life: final report to MedPAC. Washington, DC: MedPAC; 2000.

3. Wu AW, Damiano AM, Lynn J, et al. Predicting future functional status for seriously ill hospitalized adults: the SUPPORT prognostic model. *Annals of Internal Medicine*. 1995;122(5):342-350.

4. Spettell CM, Rawlins WS, Krakauer R, et al. A comprehensive case management program to improve palliative care. *Journal of Palliative Medicine*. 2009;12(9):827-832.

5. Krakauer R, Spettell CM, Reisman L, Wade MJ. Opportunities to improve the quality of care for advanced illness. *Health Affairs (Millwood)*. 2009;28(5):1357-1359.

6. Weeks WB, Nelson WA. Ethical issues arising from variation in health services utilization at the end of life. *Frontiers of Health Services Management*. 2011;27(3):17-26.

7. Krakauer R. Invictus: increasing patient choice in advanced illness and end-of-life care. *Frontiers of Health Services Management*. 2011;27(3):43-48.

ten

Focusing on the Patient's Needs and Desires: Care at Home

—Michael Fleming, MD

"Death is a continuation of life, and a friend to be prepared for."
—Joseph Cardinal Bernadin

JOSEPH CARDINAL BERNADIN already had served 13 years as Chicago's archbishop when he learned about the cancer. It was in his pancreas. Doctors removed the cancer in June of 1995 and pronounced Bernadin healthy. Soon after, Bernadin began his cancer ministry. The ministry drew an avalanche of praise, hope, and thanks from millions of sick, dying, and survivors of cancer. The ministry was more than a sounding board for cancer patients; it opened a new dialogue about death, written by those who saw it up close. They'd learned that death was a part of life, not something to run from. The archbishop was their most visible public figure.

Bernadin's cancer returned the following summer. It had spread to his liver, and this time, it was inoperable.

Bernadin traveled to Rome, put his affairs in order, and chose to face his own death in the public eye. He spoke often and openly about a subject usually deemed too sensitive. In *The Gift of Peace*,[1] a memoir he penned about it all, Bernadin wrote that death was a continuation of life and a friend to be prepared for.

Needed: A Patient-Centered Continuum of Care at Home

Data from the U.S. Department of Health and Human Services show that 6 out of 10 baby boomers, or 37 million people, will have more than one chronic condition by 2030.[2] Today, more than 10 million Medicare beneficiaries have five or more chronic conditions, and patients with chronic conditions comprise roughly one-quarter of all Medicare enrollees but account for nearly 70% of all Medicare spending.[3] The number of people with chronic conditions is growing. In fact, beneficiaries with three or more chronic conditions are the fastest-growing segment of the Medicare population.[4]

The current healthcare delivery system was built around the needs from decades ago. It is focused on facility-based care—a treat-and-cure model—and does not adequately address the current or future needs of the population. The current fee-for-service system, which pays providers for specific procedures and services rather than for the outcomes they achieve, reflects this outdated approach to care and is not sustainable.

This challenge presents an incredible opportunity for a new healthcare delivery model that consists of comprehensive and integrated **at-home** care for patients with chronic conditions, from the first diagnosis of a chronic illness (which, e.g., may require only nutrition and medication management) through care during an advanced illness, with palliative care and hospice as options.

This new care delivery model permits the provision of comprehensive services earlier in the healthcare delivery process while empowering and educating the patient. This allows the patient and family to better understand the value in all treatment options, including palliative care and hospice. Comprehensive services are provided by a broad-based team of professionals that includes medical directors, nurse practitioners, nurses, social workers, dietitians, rehabilitation professionals, spiritual counselors, and nursing aides—with the patient as the central decision maker.

What at home? Amid the high costs of healthcare and in the wake of recent healthcare reform, mounting research shows the need for a more patient-centered approach to care—one that moves the patient from a passive receiver of treatment to the role of active decision maker. The early iterations of this new model, the medical home, envisioned that care would not necessarily be provided within a doctor-based group practice or an acute setting; rather, it would be delivered to patients where they live.

As Dr. Mike Magee said in an address to the Institute of Medicine Summit on Integrative Care, "While I embrace the values of 'Medical Home,' it must be said that it is significantly underpowered to manage the future health needs of this nation. My concerns in six words: 'Too Much Medical, Not Enough Home.'"[5] Any new model of care that aligns with the continuum must focus on the patients where they reside.

The current model of care views hospitals and clinics as the center of care. However, that simply does not fit with the individual needs of patients and families in the twenty-first century. Rather than looking at discharges from the hospital as the end of a care experience, we ought to look at hospital admissions as "discharges from the community."

Research by the Public Policy Institute of the AARP found that 89% of individuals age 50 years and older want to remain in their homes as they age, including receiving treatment there. Beyond patient preference, the comforts of home have also been proven to promote healing, reduce health risks, and serve as a cost-effective option to other post–acute care settings. Additionally, healthcare at home allows clinicians to identify in-home safety hazards, medical and medication discrepancies, and social challenges not always visible in a clinical setting.

By providing care in the home, deeper, more open relationships between healthcare professionals and their patients are possible.

A Comprehensive Solution: Bringing the Continuum of Care to the Home

The Amedisys integrated care delivery model is designed to comprehensively address the individual needs of patients from early diagnosis through the care of an advanced illness, all wherever the patient calls home. This model features a team of healthcare professionals that becomes actively involved with a patient upon diagnosis and integrates a variety of disciplines throughout the care continuum, up to and including palliative care and hospice.

There are five core elements within this model: care transition, physician engagement, chronic care coordination, pharmacy management, and patient/caregiver engagement.

Care transition is designed to ensure that the patient has a smooth transition among all care settings. Patients are at their most vulnerable after discharge. In fact, one in five Medicare patients ended up back in the hospital fewer than 30 days after discharge in 2003 and 2004, according to research from the *New England Journal of Medicine*.[6] Data from Healthcare Market Resources reveal that two of the most common reasons for hospital readmissions are medication errors and failure to see a physician—both of which can be reduced with effective at-home supervision of patients following hospital discharge.[7] Unfortunately, current payment systems have not encouraged providers to coordinate a patient's care during transition from facility-based care back to the community. The passage of the Accountable Care Act (ACA) changes this paradigm.

Targeted interventions within this new model can reduce hospital readmission rates and help a group of people often unprepared to manage their own conditions.

Physician engagement is designed to close the gap between doctors who treat patients in the hospital and doctors who treat patients once they get home. With the increased number of hospitalists, a patient may be admitted and discharged from the hospital without his or her primary care doctor ever knowing. Close collaboration between hospitalists, primary care physicians, and specialists will help reduce readmissions and provide more seamless follow-up care.

Healthcare reforms started through the ACA indicate that health systems of the future must adapt to the needs of the current population and encourage the primary care physician to work closely with the patient and other healthcare partners. This new model of care provides for this coordination between physicians and patients.

Chronic care coordination takes aim at a common complaint: doctors and hospitals have a tendency to act in isolation, providing care based on incomplete information or medical history. The Amedisys model includes a detailed assessment plan that integrates patient history with social environment and home dynamics.

Pharmacy management enhances patient compliance and utilizes home care to make sure medications are taken as directed. Multiple studies have connected lower hospitalization rates with adherence to medication regimens. Cardiovascular patients who don't take their prescriptions as directed are 11% more likely to be rehospitalized,[8] and less than 40% of patients are likely to adhere to their prescription directives after two years.[8]

Patient and caregiver engagement moves patients and their caregivers from passive receivers of treatment to the role of active decision makers in their care plan. Healthcare professionals educate patients by teaching them how to self-manage their chronic diseases. At-home visits allow clinicians to see patients in their natural environment, how they live, how active they are, and the nutritional patterns of both patients and caregivers. As individuals progress through the continuum of care and eventually need to consider care for an advanced illness, they are better prepared to make decisions related to palliative and hospice care options. Patient and caregiver engagement is also about relationship building:

a foundation for trust and acceptance that often proves crucial when patients are facing advanced illnesses.

Palliative Care and Hospice

The current thought process of healthcare providers, policy makers, and even patients includes individual silos where an individual enters on one end when a diagnosis is given and comes out of the other only to reenter the same or another silo when a different need arises. This antiquated healthcare delivery model imposes a triage-and-treat system on a population that needs to be comprehensively managed.

We have to leave behind grounded beliefs that care starts and stops at definitive points in time and begin viewing the healthcare of individuals as a continuum.

As an example, palliative care marks a practical and philosophical shift in how patients view their illnesses. Treatment shifts from curing or overcoming disease to accepting and managing one's quality of life. Palliative care takes a holistic approach to relieving suffering in patients with advanced illnesses by tailoring treatment to people's values, caregiver needs, and attention to home life.

A 2010 survey from the *National Journal* "Living Well and the End of Life" poll found that "hospice" and "end-of-life care" were terms familiar to Americans, while "palliative care" was not.[9] And yet a 2010 study from the *New England Journal of Medicine* found that getting early palliative care helped people with lung cancer live three months longer, compared with those given standard care.[10] The study also found that palliative care patients enjoyed a better quality of life and caregivers were less depressed. Nearly three-quarters of those surveyed in the *National Journal* poll said it was more important to enhance the quality of life for seriously ill patients, even if it meant a shorter life.[9]

Hospice, a form of palliative care for patients in the last six months of life, has been shown to help patients live longer, ease caregiver burdens, and reduce Medicare costs. Research from *Social Science and Medicine* found that hospice use reduced Medicare costs in the last year of life by an average of about $2,300 per patient.[11] A study from the *Journal of Pain and Symptom Management* showed that hospice patients with serious cancer or congestive heart failure lived an average of 30 days longer than nonhospice patients.[12] Another study of cancer patients from the *Journal of Clinical Oncology* found that caregivers of patients who died in an intensive care unit were five times more likely to be diagnosed with posttraumatic stress disorder than caregivers of patients who died at home with hospice services.[13]

Additionally, results from 2010 Amedisys hospice satisfaction surveys found that satisfaction with hospice care ranks high with patients and caregivers. Among the findings:

- 99% said their loved one was admitted within 24 hours,
- 96% said hospice decreased anxiety and stress levels,
- 98.5% said staff involved them in decisions regarding care,
- Nearly 97% said they were pleased with the after-hours services, and
- Nearly 98% said they would recommend hospice service to others.

The impact of hospice care is not restricted to patient and family outcomes. Rather, research from Duke University validated the positive financial impact of hospice with a finding that Medicare costs are reduced for 7 out of 10 patients if hospice was used for a longer period of time. "More effort should be put into increasing short stays [in hospice]," the authors wrote, "as opposed to shortening longer ones."[11]

Despite these findings, data from NHPCO show that the median length of service for hospice care in 2009 was 21.1 days, a slight drop from 21.3 days in 2008. The average length of service decreased from 69.5 days in 2008 to 69 days in 2009. Fewer patients remained under hospice care for more than 180 days in 2009 compared with 2008.[14]

New service delivery and payment models must support these comprehensive services available at home and assist patients in choosing a different kind of healthcare model—one that includes palliative care and hospice as care options earlier in the process—allowing individuals to live out their lives as they choose.

Patient Case Study

Svante was an engineer, a strong man with a kind heart, two kids, and a 20-year smoking habit. He worked for the same company for 40-plus years and traveled the world: Sweden, the United States, South Africa. He quit smoking at age 50 and underwent bypass surgery two years later. Soon after he retired at 65, his health declined. Svante developed an aortic embolism and was having more and more trouble breathing.

By age 72, doctors suspected he likely suffered from chronic obstructive pulmonary disease, or COPD. The disease involves a combination of chronic bronchitis and emphysema, which restricts airflow to the lungs. The disease is progressive but often manageable with a combination of inhalers, supplemental oxygen, and steroid treatment. Svante would be OK. Doctors had good reason to trust their diagnosis, given his symptoms and smoking history.

Svante's wife, Kerstin, had her doubts. Born and raised in Sweden, she had immigrated to the United States by herself at age 23 with a set of health papers, little money, and a local sponsor. She raised two children and saw the world with her husband. Not one to accept a doctor's opinion on just his or her say-so, she could tell the inhalers doctors kept giving Svante those past two years weren't working. On their last trip, a cruise to South America, her husband just couldn't keep up.

Kerstin checked the Internet and learned about something called idiopathic pulmonary fibrosis, or IPD. This progressive disease attacks the lungs themselves. The soft, elastic tissue of the lungs grows thick and stiff, making it harder and harder to expand and contract. Unlike COPD, the prognosis is grim: a lifetime of supplementary oxygen and, eventually, a lung transplant. The disease ravages the lungs and turns healthy tissue into a honeycomb, until the lungs succumb to pneumonia.

The couple returned from their cruise in the spring and got a second opinion from another doctor, who confirmed it was pulmonary fibrosis. They went to a local university to see whether Svante was a candidate for a lung transplant, but his history of heart trouble disqualified him. Kerstin's husband was dying. Doctors said he likely would need hospice care by year's end.

The decision to choose hospice care can be hard for some, says Bobbie Legg, a medical social worker with 30 years of experience, including the past 6 with Amedisys. The impulse to fight disease is natural. People just want to keep trying. Bobbie also acknowledges public perception—that choosing hospice care is tantamount to "giving up"—but says that idea is rooted in fear. Also, many patients and their families view hospice care as "less" care—when, in fact, hospice care represents the very best of truly patient-centered care.

Individuals with advanced illness, along with their caregivers, will more likely be receptive to hospice care when they have been engaged and active participants throughout the entire process.

Instead of seeing hospice as "giving up," Bobbie says it's really a time for patients to make key decisions about their own quality of life. Empower them as active decision makers instead of "patients who receive care," she says, and the fear will fade.

Kerstin's husband did some pulmonary rehab during the summer. Year's end came and went. The couple signed up for home health services with Amedisys in December but so far had used them mainly for physical therapy and in-home nurse care.

Then, on April 30, Kerstin's husband fell and hit his head.

He was rushed to the hospital, where doctors decided it was best to stop testing and recommended home hospice. Kerstin recalls her husband asking her, "Do I have a choice?"

"Sure," she said. "You can stay here or go home."

"He said he wanted to go home, and that was good," Kerstin recalls. "I felt it was best for everybody to be at home, where he was in our bedroom in familiar surroundings."

Kerstin's husband was transferred home. Bobbie Legg was among the team that included a home hospice nurse, a hospice aid, a physical therapist, a registered nurse, and a chaplain. Svante's son and daughter both came home to be with their dad. His daughter, Susanne, says she's glad her dad got to make his own choice.

"It was up to him to decide how he wanted to continue his life," Susanne says. "Did he want to stay in a hospital to see if there were things they could do to make him better there, or did he want to go home? Based on his decision, it seemed like a good way to go. Having care at home, where you have all your personal items instead of a hospital, which is so much more impersonal, I think is probably the best decision for everyone."

Bobbie recalls the day Svante's hospice bed was delivered to his home. It was a big day. A world traveler, Svante liked to look out the window and watch the day's sky change with time. He also kept current by watching the news on TV.

"The bed was a big change for him," Bobbie recalls. "The whole family got involved and thought, 'How can we rearrange the room so he has the best view out the window and can watch the news?' Everything was out there, discussed openly. He was an active participant in this process, and that was a real joy to see."

An animal lover, Svante spent part of his last few days playing with his son's cat, a black tom named Vader. Svante lived at home for 18 days before he died. It was a Tuesday.

Conclusion

According to the Congressional Budget Office, rising costs, especially under Medicare and Medicaid, are the single greatest threat to the country's economic stability.[15] Therefore, whichever way the political winds happen to blow in coming years, healthcare cost containment will continue to be a major focus for decades to come.

Healthcare reforms started with the Accountable Care Act depend on the fact that health systems of the future adapt to the needs of the current population, a population where the number of patients with serious or terminal illness is the fastest-growing segment of the Medicare population.

The model outlined within this chapter addresses the needs of this exact population, and it is through the use of such models that better healthcare can be provided to more individuals at a lower cost. It defines a model that aligns with the Institute of Medicine's goal of healthcare to "deliver the right care for the right patient at the right time, all of the time."

Melanie Gibson, regional director of operations for Amedisys, concedes that palliative care and hospice need to be a bigger part of the conversation before this monumental shift in healthcare delivery can take place. Healthcare delivery with a payment system that allows for the provision of services based on the patient's needs much earlier on in the diagnosis has the ability to truly be a patient-centered medical home.

⸎

Michael Fleming, MD, joined Amedisys as chief medical officer in 2009. Dr. Fleming brings more than 29 years of medical field experience to his new position. He is past president of the American Academy of Family Physicians and the Louisiana Academy of Family Physicians and was founding president of the Louisiana Health Care Quality Forum, a partnership with the State of Louisiana aiming to provide high-quality healthcare to the state. Dr. Fleming has served as speaker of the Congress of Delegates of the AAFP and as board chair of the AAFP Board of Directors. As an active member of the medical quality field, he serves on various boards and panels to the health information technology industry. Additionally, he participates in international activities promoting medical education and primary care worldwide. Dr. Fleming continues his role as founding director, chairman, and chief medical officer for Antidote Education Company, producing continuing education for healthcare providers. He serves as an assistant clinical professor in the Department of Family Medicine at Louisiana State University Health Science Center and in the Department of Family and Community Medicine at Tulane University Medical School. Dr. Fleming was honored as Louisiana Family Doctor of the Year in 1996. The LSU Health Science Center presented him with the Family Medicine Award upon graduation in 1975; in 2003 the award was renamed and is now called the Michael O. Fleming Award in Family Medicine.

References

1.   Bernardin J. *The gift of peace: personal reflections.* Chicago: Loyola Press; 1997.

2.   US Department of Health and Human Services. Secretary Sebelius awards funding for chronic disease self-management programs for older Americans. http://www. hhs.gov/news/press/2010pres/03/20100330a.html. Accessed September 8, 2011.

3.   Anderson GF. Medicare and chronic conditions. *New England Journal of Medicine.* 2005;353(3):305-309. Paez KA, Zhao L, Hwang W. Rising out-of-pocket spending for chronic conditions: a ten-year trend. *Health Affairs (Millwood).* 2009;28(1):15-25.

4.   Magee M. Address to the Institute of Medicine Summit on Integrative Medicine and the Health of the Public, February 25–27, 2009. http://imsummitweb cast. org/. Accessed September 8, 2011.

5.   Magee M, Minnix WL, Dishman E. *Home-centered health care: the populist transformation of the American health care system.* New York: Spencer Books; 2007.

6.   Jencks SF, Williams MV, Coleman EA. Rehospitalizations among patients in the Medicare fee-for-service program. *New England Journal of Medicine.* 2009;360(14):1418-1428.

7.   Too many patients are going home from the hospital unsupervised. *Market Research Letter.* January–February 2011. http://www.healthmr.com/resources/newsletter-archive/1101-metrics-matter. Accessed September 8, 2011.

8.   Living well at the end of life: a national conversation. *National Journal* Web site. http://syndication.nationaljournal.com/communications/ NationalJournalRegenceToplines.pdf. Accessed October 15, 2011.

9.   Temel JS, Greer JA, Muzikansky A, et al. Early palliative care for patients
     with metastatic non-small-cell lung cancer. *New England Journal of Medicine.*
     2010;363(8):733-742.

10. Taylor DH Jr, Ostermann J, Van Houtven CH, Tulsky JA, Steinhauser K. What
     length of hospice use maximizes reduction in medical expenditures near death in
     the US Medicare program? *Social Science and Medicine.* 2007;65(7):1466-1478.

11. Connor SR, Pyenson B, Fitch K, Spence C, Iwasaki K. Comparing hospice and
     nonhospice patient survival among patients who die within a three-year window.
     Journal of Pain and Symptom Management. 2007;33(3):238-246.

12. Akechi T, Okuyama T, Sugawara Y, Nakano T, Shima Y, Uchitomi Y. Major
     depression, adjustment disorders, and post-traumatic stress disorder in terminally
     ill cancer patients: associated and predictive factors. *Journal of Clinical Oncology.*
     2004;22(10):1957-1965.

13. NHPCO facts and figures: hospice care in America. Alexandria, VA: National
     Hospice and Palliative Care Organization, September 2010. http://www.nhpco.
     org/files/public/Statistics_Research/Hospice_Facts_ Figures_Oct-2010.pdf.
     Accessed September 8, 2011.

14. Congress of the US Congressional Budget Office. *The budget and economic outlook:
     fiscal years 2010 to 2020,* January 2010, p. 21. http://www.cbo.gov/ftpdocs /108xx/
     doc10871/01-26-Outlook.pdf. Accessed September 8, 2011.

Section III

Perspectives of Persons Receiving Care

IN SECTIONS I and II of this book, the authors, all of whom are connected with healthcare, have used many stories to clarify and explain how a different model of care for their patients with advanced illness leads to better care. But what do the individuals and families who receive this care think? Ultimately, for this new model of care to have value, it must be seen and felt by the people with advanced illness and by the families who help support them.

In this section, we will address this question by hearing from patients who are facing serious illness and from families who had to make decisions for loved ones. Through these stories we hear how the chance to think about and plan for future medical decisions provided an opportunity to make informed decisions about what makes sense for the ill person. We will also hear from two family members and see how this planning helped them address difficult decisions and ultimately the grief from the death of their loved one. Finally, we will have a comprehensive report from two authors from the American Association of Retired Persons (AARP), Naomi Karp and Lynn Friss Feinburg, who review survey data from Americans. In their chapter we learn what Americans think about care of those with advanced illness, what Americans would want from the care system, and how we might best meet these expectations.

What we learn from these voices is that Americans want a say in what care they get and that they prefer to have this care delivered in a way that helps them function as well as possible, close to those they love, addressing issues of both distress and comfort. They don't want to be denied care that will help them, but they also don't want to undergo treatment that will cause great burden and has little benefit while also creating financial hardship.

eleven

The Value of Advance Care Planning: Perspectives from Patients and Families

WHETHER UNEXPECTED OR after a long illness, when a loved one nears the end of life, it is an emotional time for family members. If family members do not know what their loved one would want, those emotions can be further heightened. Healthcare providers often see the angst, fear, second-guessing, and guilt that family members can experience. On the other hand, when a patient has an advance care plan and conversations with family members have taken place, the experience, while sad, can also be peaceful.

The people who share their stories here have different backgrounds and experiences. Some have lost loved ones and have seen firsthand the value of advance care planning. Others have put together their own plans so their loved ones are prepared should anything happen to them. They all share their stories in the hope that they will inspire others.

A Critical Conversation

As told by Jeff Lokken

Jeff Lokken is a native of La Crosse, Wisconsin, and lives near Holmen, Wisconsin, with his family. A wealth manager by trade, Jeff discusses the importance of planning for the future with his clients and encourages them to plan not only for decisions that will need to be made about their finances but also for healthcare decisions that may need to be made for them. He didn't know how vital those healthcare plans would become for his own family.

MY PARENTS, JOHN and Marie Lokken, weren't the type of people to talk about personal issues, such as finances or their healthcare decisions. As they got older, though, they recognized the importance of having a plan in place if medical decisions needed to be made and they weren't able to speak for themselves.

In the early '90s, my parents first sat down with an advance care planning facilitator at Gundersen Health System to start the conversations that would lead to the creation of their advance directives. It was an important step because it gave us reference points for all of our future conversations. They sat down with me, as their medical power of attorney, to talk about their goals, their plans, and their wishes. We had no idea at the time how critical those discussions would become later in their lives.

Our family's first experience with an advance directive came with Dad. He had been sick with throat cancer and other illnesses over the years. Then, in 1999, he got an infection after open-heart surgery. It became clear to all of us that the outcome would not be what we had hoped.

A couple of days before he died, Dad looked at me and said, "I don't think this is going to go well. Let's go through everything." We sat in his hospital room and went through his advance directive line by line, and we talked about his wishes and whether anything had changed. He wasn't one to talk about it often, but when he did, he was very direct and deliberate.

Dad's attitude was "If I can get better, do whatever you need to do to fix me. If I can't get better, don't prolong my life." Dad went quickly downhill, and when it became clear to the doctors and to us that he would not recover, we made the decision as a family to remove him from the ventilator. It was what he wanted.

There was no second-guessing, no "what-ifs." It was still astonishingly traumatic when he passed away, but my brothers, sisters, and I knew it was the right decision. We had talked about it and planned many years beforehand. While the decision itself is never easy, the process was made simpler, and we didn't have to hesitate. We did what we knew Dad wanted us to do.

Mom's experience was very different, but the end result was the same: her wishes were respected at the end of her life. A lifelong smoker, Mom had advanced lung disease and was in a nursing home the last five years of her life. There were many times in those five years we thought we would lose her, but she was incredibly resilient.

Unlike Dad's initial reaction in creating his plan, Mom's was "Do whatever you need to do to keep me alive as long as possible." As the years went on, though, her feelings changed, and her advance directive changed. We had many conversations where we reviewed the document, and it changed a little bit more each time. In the end, she didn't want machines keeping her alive. Her goal was simply to be made as comfortable as possible when she passed away. She was in control, and her death, like her life, was very dignified.

It is so important to plan ahead. If the time comes when you need to make a decision for your loved one, you do not want to be guessing. You have to be prepared, and you have to have reference points so you know what to do if your loved one can no longer speak for himself or herself. We were fortunate in our case because my parents created their advance directives long before they were needed. We were able to review them, and as my parents' wishes changed, we modified their advance directives.

Even more important than the document, though, is the conversation that surrounds it. To me, the conversation is critical. You cannot just hand someone a document. You need to talk about it, explain your thoughts, and have a dialogue. If you are the medical power of attorney, you need to ask questions and get a deeper understanding of what your loved one means about the statements in the document. None of us lives forever, so it's not crazy to have these conversations—it's necessary. I found the conversations to be so important that I took my adult daughter along for one of the meetings to review Mom's advance directive. I wanted her to see the process firsthand, become familiar with it, and not fear it.

For families who haven't had conversations or when an advance directive isn't available, I'm sure the choices that need to be made at the end of life are overwhelming. Not knowing whether you did the right thing can lead to feelings of guilt. As we came to the end of my parents' lives, we were fortunate. We'd had conversations. There was no second-guessing.

Today, I often mention advance care planning to my wealth management clients. They are usually in their older years, and I encourage them to talk to their healthcare provider and start the conversation with their family. I share the experience I had with my parents with them and tell them how fortunate we felt as a family that our parents had an advance directive and that we'd had these conversations ahead of time. We knew we did what was right—and what they wanted—and it made all the difference.

One of the Most Important Conversations We Had

As told by Greg Loomis

Greg Loomis was one of the primary caregivers helping his father prior to his father's passing. Greg helped his father maintain independence for the last few years of his life. Having experienced the

benefits of facilitated advance care planning conversations with his
father, he shares his story in hopes it will make a difference in the
lives of others.

WHEN MY FATHER passed away in 2010, he was 96 years old. He taught me a lot during those 96 years, but some of the greatest lessons came in the last few years of his life.

Dad was a fiercely independent person. Even at 96, he was living on his own in a senior housing center in Onalaska, Wisconsin, and driving himself to the dialysis unit at Gundersen Health System, where he was receiving treatment for kidney failure. He valued his independence and did not want to give up his car. In his head, he did not want to burden any of us.

Over the years, I spoke to him about the "what-ifs," such as "What if you fell?" "What if you had a stroke?" "What if you got into a car accident?" etc. I had a general idea of what my father preferred, but we never put anything in writing.

When my father's health got past the point of just dialysis, he realized he needed to listen to the healthcare providers. He scheduled an appointment to sit down with an advance care planning facilitator at Gundersen Health System and begin taking the steps to create an advance directive. We both sat down together and met with the facilitator. This was one of the most important conversations I had with my father.

The conversation was eye-opening for me. With a third party present, I learned things I never knew about my dad—not only his wishes for his healthcare but also things about his career and how he raised his children. What became very clear throughout the conversation was that Dad never wanted to go to a nursing home—he considered it the "kiss of death," and he did not want to put himself in that place. He also did not want a drawn-out death. Looking back, I see that this was very critical.

During the conversation with the facilitator, she asked a lot of questions and presented choices to my father. She stuck to the facts and told him what options were available. At no point was there any pressure to choose one option or another. Instead, it was like a multiple-choice test, and no answer was the wrong answer. The choice was his; the facilitation just provided the road map.

That meeting triggered multiple follow-up conversations with my father. The last few years of his life we had more father-son talks than we did for the first 60 years of my life. I wish I could have had those types of conversations earlier.

In the end, my father suffered a massive stroke. When it became clear he would not recover, my brothers and I gathered together and discussed the wishes Dad laid out in his advance directive. We all knew he did not want life-sustaining treatment. The decision was not up to us; our father made it very clear what he wanted in advance.

This experience with my father in his late years allowed me to develop my own advance directive when I was in my 50s and share my wishes with my family. During a recent surgery, my care team was surprised to see an advance directive already in place. My dad was fortunate that he was blessed with 96 years, as you never know what tomorrow will bring. It makes you stop and think about the potential stress levels on many families when those advance directives are not created; it makes you think about what happens if a loved one is in an accident or experiences a sudden heart attack or stroke and there is no plan in place. Not only are you struggling to recover from the initial shock of the accident but also you are then put in a stressful place when trying to make a decision for someone else. It really makes you want to be proactive and potentially alleviate some of the burden.

To me, the beauty of an advance directive is that it can always be changed. It's a journey. I know that what I wanted at 52 or 62 may not be the same thing that I want when I am 92. I will continue to review my advance directive every few years and update it if necessary, to make it easier for my family.

It's a lesson I learned from my dad, and for that, I will always be grateful.

An Eye-Opening Experience

As told by Arlene Schumacher

Ed and Arlene Schumacher live in the home where they raised their family in rural Minnesota, about 20 minutes from La Crosse, Wisconsin. At 92 and 89 years old, respectively, they have remained independent and enjoy the peace and quiet their country home provides. Ed, a World War II veteran, worked as a carpenter most of his life. He suffers from advanced lung disease and participates in Gundersen Health System's Advanced Disease Coordination program. His care providers encouraged both Ed and Arlene to consider creating advance directives. They were guided through the process by a facilitator at Gundersen Health System. Arlene shares what the experience was like for them.

ED AND I had never really thought much about having an advance directive. We'd talked from time to time about what we wanted if it came to that, but we never put anything down in writing or in our medical records. The importance of an advance directive was brought to the forefront in 2010 when Ed was hospitalized the first of many times in a short period.

In July, Ed was at a baseball game in Stewartville, Minnesota, and passed out. I was home getting ready for a wedding at the time, so it was a shock to learn he'd been taken to the hospital. He was in the hospital for three days that time. He had a number of episodes after that and ended up in the hospital another three times before December. The last time he was in the hospital, his doctor talked to him about the Advanced Disease Coordination program at Gundersen Health System and palliative care. He has lung disease and other health problems, and his doctor thought it would be good for him to work with a team to coordinate his care, help him determine what "living well" meant to him, and develop a plan to meet his needs.

When we met with his care team, they asked whether we had advance directives. When we said no, they helped us get the process started. With the health problems Ed was having at the time, it made us realize this was something important for us to do and not put off any longer.

We sat down with the facilitator, Carol, and had a long conversation. She asked Ed a lot of questions and talked to him about some of the decisions he would need to make, such as whether he would want cardiopulmonary resuscitation (CPR) if he stopped breathing and his heart stopped beating. I learned that CPR is something Ed would want for himself, and he learned it's not something I want. If my heart stops beating, I want him to let me go. We talked about different situations, and Ed thought about each one and what he would want to happen if he experienced it.

Creating the plan solidified much of what I thought I knew about Ed. I know that if he will not be able to sit and have a conversation—"If I'm going to be a vegetable," as he puts it—he doesn't want care that will keep him here. I know that he wants a military funeral because he's proud of his service in the army, and we've even talked about a poem he wants read at his funeral.

The process of sitting down with Carol and putting together Ed's plan made us aware of where we are in life. We're not going to live forever, and some of these decisions have to be made. It's something that needs to be talked about. By creating an advance directive, Ed was able to make the right decisions for himself. I won't be forced and my children won't be forced to make those decisions for him. I, too, have now created an advance directive so Ed and our children will know my wishes.

Creating our advance directives was an eye-opener. I'm glad we did it.

Realizing the Importance of Planning Ahead
As told by Evie Herold

Evie Herold and her husband, Jim, live in an apartment complex for seniors in the small community of Brownsville, Minnesota. Married for 22 years, Evie and Jim had not had any discussions about their wishes if healthcare decisions needed to be made for them and they could not speak for themselves. At 79 years old, Evie has multiple health concerns and began working with Gundersen Health System Advanced Disease Coordination specialists and palliative care in 2011. During a discussion with a palliative care coordinator, Evie first learned about advance care planning.

IN THE SPRING of 2011, my doctor suggested that I start working with a coordinator in palliative care. I have several health issues—my heartbeat is irregular, and I've struggled with blood clots for a number of years—and she wanted to make sure I had other people on my care team who could work with me alongside her.

During one of my meetings with Marsha, my palliative care coordinator, she mentioned advance care planning. It wasn't something I'd really thought about or knew about until she brought it up. When she explained what it was all about, I thought, "That's a really good idea." Marsha helped us coordinate a time for a facilitator, Carol, to come out to our home and sit down with me and my husband, Jim, to begin creating an advance directive.

Our time with Carol was wonderful. It felt like we were sitting and talking to someone we'd known a long time. She made us feel so comfortable. As we talked, she asked us a lot of questions that really made us think. I know Jim learned some things about my wishes that surprised him, such as the fact that I want to donate my organs when I pass away. Even though it's on my driver's license, it's not something I'd ever told him. While we created my advance care plan and

Jim's, too, Carol walked us through everything and made sure we understood the decisions we were making.

The experience was a wonderful one for us and made us wonder why we didn't do it sooner! I've had many surgeries over the years, and anything could have happened. My family would have been put in a position to make decisions for me, and that's so hard. Jim experienced it with his first wife. She was brain-dead, and Jim and his children had to make a decision on whether she should be taken off the respirator. It is so hard on the family to make that decision, and they hadn't had conversations with her to know what she would have wanted. I would hate to put Jim in the same situation. Now he knows what I want.

Before we sat down with Carol, Jim and I had never talked about what we would want to happen in different situations. It feels so much better to have had those conversations. Since we sat down with Carol, I've talked to one of my daughters, who will also act as my healthcare agent if she's needed. She's now aware of the decisions I made in my advance directive.

After going through the process, I realize how important it is to plan ahead. I've encouraged many of our friends and neighbors to talk to their healthcare providers about getting started on an advance care plan. In the end, it would make things so much easier on your spouse, your children, your family. I just think everybody should have one, period.

A Rainbow of Support

As told by Ruth Nixon Davy

Ruth Nixon Davy is a retired professor who taught Spanish at the University of Wisconsin–La Crosse for 39 years. Today, she is an independent 95-year-old who lives alone in an assisted living facility in La Crosse. With many of her longtime healthcare providers retiring, Ruth decided to take part in Gundersen Health

System's Advanced Disease Coordination program, which includes palliative care. Even before taking part in the program, Ruth had many conversations with her daughter-in-law, Joyce, who is her healthcare agent, about her future wishes and what it means for her to "live well."

WHEN MY DOCTOR first recommended palliative care and the Advanced Disease Coordination program, I didn't know what it was. Joyce and I both thought palliative care was something for people who don't have long to live. We thought maybe we missed something along the way! My doctor quickly explained that the program is not just for people who are in hospice or have a terminal illness. The team is there to help me manage my healthcare and live as well as I can.

I don't have what I consider "real bad" health problems, but over the years I've developed some health issues that require monitoring. I have an aneurysm around my heart, and in 1996 I had a heart valve replaced with a calf valve. Vertigo can also cause problems for me from time to time, so I've had a couple of serious falls.

As I first sat down with the palliative care coordinator, she took time to get to know me. She asked a lot of questions about my life and how I wanted to live from now until the time that I die. After she got to know me a little bit, we talked more specifically about different situations that I could encounter in the future. We talked about what I would want to have happen if I have a stroke, for example, or if I fall again and break bones. I told her that I don't want things done to me just to keep me alive. I want to still have some quality of life, be able to sit on a couch and have a conversation, and stay in assisted living or a nursing home, if it comes to that. We made changes to my advance directive so my wishes are spelled out for different situations.

Joyce and I have had many conversations over the years about my wishes and what I want as I live out the rest of my days. She says it's comforting to her to know what I want because it gives closure on what she should do if it comes to that.

To me, conversations are so very important, and I've had those conversations with Joyce, with the medical professionals at Gundersen Health System, and with the people here at my assisted living home. They all have copies of my advance directive, and they know my wishes.

While I haven't been part of the palliative care program long, I think it is a wonderful thing. It is like a rainbow of sorts—a light that's there to guide you along the way, with many colors to it that change as your needs change. I appreciate the extra support. It is good to be a part of it.

twelve

How Do Older People and Their Families Benefit from Advance Care Planning and Support?

—Naomi Karp, JD, and Lynn Friss Feinberg, MSW

NEARLY EVERYONE OF a certain age has had experience with serious or advanced illness, care near the end of life, or the death of a loved one. Sometimes these experiences—especially when family members feel unprepared or excluded from the decision-making process or see their family member suffer and wonder why—catalyze us to think about, talk about, and plan for our own future care when illness and incapacity may strike. As writer Jane Gross says, "We have the opportunity to watch what happens to our parents, listen to what they have to say to us, and use that information to look squarely at our own mortality and prepare as best we can for the end of our own lives."[1] But sometimes these experiences leave us feeling powerless and fearful; we know what may lie ahead, but because we don't know how to make it better, we avoid concrete thought or action.

We choose to "endure the experience until it's over and then escape back into the daily buzz of our lives until suddenly it's our turn."[1]

With the aging of the population and the increasing number of Americans living with serious and complex chronic conditions, more families will be faced with profound caregiving and advanced illness realities in the future. In addition, with the growing incidence of Alzheimer's disease, other dementias, and other causes of cognitive impairment, more and more people will be unable to make or communicate treatment choices, at least for some period of their lives or their illnesses. Preparing and supporting people with advanced illness and their families will become even more important to society as the baby boomers reach old age and constraints on public financing for healthcare and long-term care continue to mount.

Effective advance care planning—and professional and community support for older adults and their families—can move us toward a paradigm in which people accept the realities of aging, disease, and death. With workable and evidence-based models for communication, planning, documentation, and care delivery, people can collaborate with healthcare and social service providers as they or their family members move through the trajectory of advancing illness. As we move toward these goals—and we educate the public and professionals about how to take steps in that direction—we can hope to diminish some of that fear that it will be a painful time of life while encouraging realistic hopes and expectations.

What We Know about How People View Advanced Illness and Planning

Our culture is determined to defy aging and deny death. People spend untold millions on antiaging remedies, and medical researchers and drug and device manufacturers develop an astounding, ever-changing set of pharmaceuticals and technologies to keep us alive. And it is not just consumers who pursue perpetual youth and eternal life—we have allies in the medical profession.

Dr. Atul Gawande described the doctor's view: "The simple view is that medicine exists to fight death and disease, and that is, of course, its most basic task. Death is the enemy. But the enemy has superior forces. Eventually, it wins."[2]

So how do Americans view advanced illness care and advance care planning? Recent surveys give us some insight.

Most Americans have personal experience with advanced illness care, for themselves or a family member. Only half feel prepared for the experience.[3] People aged 65 years and older feel somewhat more prepared, and African Americans and Hispanics feel the most unprepared, according to a 2011 national poll.

Americans have big worries about treatment for serious illness. Several surveys identified these major concerns:[3,4]

- The cost of treatment if they or a family member becomes seriously ill,
- Not having enough information about treatment options—and especially the concern that doctors might not provide all treatment options or choices available or might not choose the best treatment option,
- Insufficient time talking with doctors and having doctors listen to them and their family,
- Not having enough control over treatment options, and
- Being a burden on their family if they become seriously ill.

The American public wants information about a range of advanced illness care options, including hospice, palliative care, and advance directives. While they worry about whether doctors will fully inform them about specific treatment options, they view doctors and other healthcare providers, as well as social service agencies, as trusted sources of information about palliative and end-of-life care.[3]

Americans think end-of-life care and hospice care should be top priorities for the healthcare system. While most don't recognize the term "palliative care," when educated about it, they think it should be a priority and would likely consider using it for themselves or a loved one.[3]

How you define "palliative care" has a big impact on how people react to the term. A definition that gets a positive response from the American public is:

> Palliative care is specialized medical care for people with
> serious illnesses. This type of care is focused on providing
> patients with relief from the symptoms, pain, and stress of a
> serious illness—whatever the diagnosis.
>
> The goal is to improve quality of life for both the patient
> and the family. Palliative care is provided by a team of doctors,
> nurses, and other specialists who work with a patient's other
> doctors to provide an extra layer of support. Palliative care is
> appropriate at any age and at any stage in a serious illness and
> can be provided together with curative treatment.[5]

Americans think about advanced illness care and the type of care they might want if they are unable to communicate their choices. But they don't always discuss these preferences with family members or friends, and they put these preferences in written documents even less frequently. Research findings on the frequency of advance care conversations and on advance directives vary but show that a minority of Americans put their preferences in writing.

- In a 2007 poll, AARP found that only 29% of adults completed an advance directive (living will or healthcare proxy). For those 60 years and older, 51% had advance directives.[6] Other literature on advance directive use reports much lower prevalence.[7]
- Nonwhite racial and ethnic groups are less likely to support the use of advance directives.[8]
- A 2010 national survey found that 57% of adults made their wishes known for healthcare treatment to prolong their life if unable to communicate due to serious illness or accident, either through informal

talks with family and friends or in writing.[9] For those aged 65 years and up, the numbers were higher, not surprisingly.

- Among boomer women age 45–64 years, more than half had thought about long-term care options, but only 45% had prepared an advance directive, according to a 2010 AARP survey.[10]

Americans often feel unprepared to make decisions on behalf of family members or others who can no longer speak or decide for themselves and experience enormous stress when called on to make decisions.[11]

What We Know about Families, Caregiving, and Advance Planning

Families are the most important source of support to older adults and people with chronic conditions or disabilities, including loved ones with serious and advanced illness. Across all ethnic groups, family care is the most preferred and trusted source of assistance.[12]

Family members often undertake caregiving willingly, and many find it rewarding, meaningful, and a way to give back to their family member, partner, or close friend. An estimated 83% of Americans say they would feel obligated to help their parent in a time of need.[13]

While caregiving for a loved one with serious illness can be intensely personal and profoundly meaningful, it is also complicated and hard work, and it is stressful. Family members can experience overwhelming anxiety about suffering, financial worries, death, and loss. The effects of providing family care can last for many years after care responsibilities have ended.

Family members who provide care to people with chronic or disabling conditions are themselves at risk. Emotional, physical, and financial problems arise from the complexities and strains of caring for loved ones with serious illness. Family caregivers are more prone to develop chronic conditions and illnesses of their own, especially as they get older. They are likely to experience depression.

Most caregivers rate their own health lower than noncaregivers.[14] With longer life spans, we can expect to see more aging baby boomers in their 60s or 70s with chronic conditions of their own caring for a parent age 90 years and older.

The economic value of the unpaid contributions of family caregivers is huge—including caregivers for people with advanced illness. The AARP Public Policy Institute recently estimated that in 2009, about 42.1 million family caregivers in the United States provided care to an adult with limitations in daily activities (such as bathing, dressing) at any given time and that about 61.6 million provided care at some time during the year. The estimated economic value of their unpaid contributions was approximately $450 billion in 2009, up from an estimated $375 billion in 2007.[15] Without family caregivers, spending for healthcare and long-term care would be much higher than the economic costs of care now. While few studies have estimated the economic value of family care specifically for persons with advanced illness, one study showed that older adults who died in the community received an average of nearly 66 hours per week of family care in the last year of life. The estimated economic value of this family care ranged from $22,514 to $42,351 per individual.[16]

One of the most difficult and heart-wrenching challenges is to make medical care decisions in the event of loss of capacity for a loved one facing serious and advanced illness. The vast majority of the public (74%) believes that when an individual has advanced illness and is unable to communicate his or her wishes about medical care, the responsibility rests with a family member.[17] Research has shown that although older people want family members involved in their healthcare decision-making process, the family members are generally not well informed and unprepared to take on this role.[18]

Older adults often talk with their adult children in advance about preferences for medical care, but many have not. Among older adults (age 65 years and older) with at least one living child, nearly two in three (63%) say they have talked to their adult children about their values and preferences for medical care if they could no longer make their own decisions; about one-third (35%) have not had this conversation with their adult children, however. Among those older adults who say they have discussed advance care planning with their adult children, 70% say they initiated the conversation, while only 10% say their adult children broached the subject. Older adults say they are more likely to have discussed with their adult children whether they have a will and what to do with family belongings (76%) than they are to have had a conversation about advanced illness care.[19] And while many report talking to their children about preferences, we don't know whether they communicate enough information to enable their children to decide when faced with specific choices along the trajectory of illness.

Family caregivers feel burdened by making surrogate decisions when they don't know what their older relative or close friend would want. Knowing a loved one's expressed values, goals, and preferences for care if he or she can no longer participate in medical decision making can provide a great sense of relief for family members and can help to avoid heartache and negative emotional burden in the future. Research has shown that discussing care preferences in advance of decisional incapacity decreases caregiver burden and can increase confidence among surrogate decision makers that they are making decisions based on care recipients' preferences.[20] For the older adult with advanced illness, it can be comforting to know that his or her personal preferences and wishes have been heard.

Toward a Workable Person—and Family—Centered Approach to Advance Care Planning

What people want and need

Public opinion research tells us a lot about what people want when they or their loved ones face serious illness. As discussed above, these wants and needs include

- Information about treatment options;
- A full range of options, including hospice and palliative care;
- Control over treatment options;

- More time talking with doctors or other health professionals about the choices facing them or their loved ones;
- An understanding of their loved one's wishes and preferences, if they must make decisions for someone unable to speak or decide about healthcare;
- Guidance on how to make decisions for someone else; and
- Support in their role as caregiver.

As we try varying approaches to planning for and coping with advanced illness, experience has helped us develop strategies to better meet these wants and needs.

Advance care planning

How can we enable people to express their preferences for future care and give them some modicum of assurance that they'll get care consistent with their goals? We've evolved a communicative approach to advance care planning that will serve us better than the earlier legal model centered on living will documents. Geriatrician Muriel Gillick describes advance care planning:

> It's a complicated enterprise that begins with clarifying the person's overall health, then moves on to determine the goals of care—what is most important at that point in time—and then seeks to translate those goals into a plan of action. What I have learned by doing this with hundreds of patients and their families, as well as by studying and writing about it, is that it is a process . . . [it's] not about completing a form, it's about discussing prognosis, it's about explaining what medical interventions can and cannot achieve and the burdens associated with them, and it's about factoring the patient's values and preferences into this complex discussion.[21]

As described by Gillick, the process sounds tailor-made to address Americans' concerns about getting enough information, getting "face time" with their doctors, making plans, and getting the care they need.

Effective advance care planning recognizes that the process is iterative. An individual's goals of care change as health declines and he or she confronts new realities of daily living. As illnesses or disabilities worsen, people may put more emphasis on "caring" than on "curing"—and palliative care can become a critical part of the plan, improving quality of life and even extending life in some cases.[22] Advance care planning is not a one-stop shop but rests on revisiting plans through continued conversations between clinicians, patients, family members, and legally authorized surrogates if the patient can no longer make decisions. And, to be meaningful, these conversations must have depth, be grounded in the realities of the person's health status, and include an understanding of life-sustaining treatment options in the context of the individual's diagnosis and disease progression. "If I'm in a coma someday, pull the plug" is not an advance care plan that will allow clear and unburdened decision making on behalf of a particular person at a particular time.

Healthcare powers of attorney, more than living wills, remain critically important, giving people assurance that the person they trust will stand in their shoes as needed. But these proxies, who are charged with honoring the person's wishes whenever possible, often don't know what their loved one would have wanted, in general or in the specific situation. When combined with a thorough advance care planning process, the proxy document can ensure that we have the right decision maker and the best possible road map for coping with advanced illness. But questions remain: How will the plan be documented? How will the documented plan change as diagnoses and prognoses evolve? How do we know that all healthcare providers in all settings in our complex and fragmented care system will know about the plan and honor it?

POLST

A strategy called POLST—Physician Orders for Life-Sustaining Treatment—aims to address those concerns for patients with advanced progressive illness and/or frailty. POLST is a tool for translating an individual's goals of care into medical orders in a highly visible, portable way. Healthcare professionals discuss with the seriously ill person (or his or her surrogate) the available treatment options in light of his or her current condition and help clarify the person's preferences. Then clinicians document those preferences on a standardized medical order form, usually in an eye-catching bright color, and ensure that the order travels with the person if he or she changes settings of care (e.g., nursing home to hospital or home to nursing home). POLST differs from an advance directive in that it is an actionable medical order dealing with the here-and-now needs of people. It can build on an advance directive but can be created for people without advance directives.[23]

POLST enables people to choose from a full range of care options, from aggressive treatment to limited interventions to comfort care. Carefully designed research documents POLST's success in improving the documentation and honoring of individual preferences, whatever they may be. Management of pain and symptoms remains comparable to that of persons without POLST.[24]

About a quarter of the states now use this protocol statewide, and most of the remaining states are looking at implementing it. It has different names and acronyms in different states, for example, POST, MOST, MOLST, and COLST.

POLST has made a great leap forward from traditional advance directives in documenting the current, real-time preferences of people in language that is recognized and honored within our medical system. But the key premise of POLST is that it is based on meaningful discussion between people (or surrogate decision makers) and their healthcare providers, thus resulting in documentation of truly informed decisions. Herein lies the challenge. The conversation that forms the basis for the POLST form must accomplish what Dr. Gillick described: discuss diagnosis and prognosis, explain what medical interventions can and cannot achieve, describe the burdens associated with them, and tie choices to the person's goals of care. Key stakeholders in the POLST program from around the country agree that this important issue is an ongoing test of POLST's success. Ongoing professional education—about communication skills and the therapeutic impact of life-sustaining interventions—has been highlighted as a key strategy for improving the quality of the conversation.[23]

Improving communication among clinicians, people with advancing illness, and their families

Improving communication—an essential component to effective advance care planning that results in a better experience for people and their loved ones—must focus on two things: the communications skills, styles, and strategies of doctors and other healthcare providers and effective tools for communicating accurate "medical facts."

Researchers such as Duke University's Dr. James Tulsky have developed insight on and interventions to enhance communication skills for advanced illness care. The research focuses on physicians, but the key points apply to other providers in our healthcare delivery system. Key elements of communication, says Tulsky,[25] include:

- **Trust.** Physicians must inspire confidence that one's healthcare provider "is acting unfailingly in one's interest." This is particularly challenging in a hospital setting when a medical team and a patient have no established relationship. Style is key: an empathic, person-centered style and a forum that permits open discussion.

- **Uncertainty.** Uncertainty characterizes all medical decision making, and physicians and other healthcare and social service providers must help people manage it. Physicians have the challenge of finding the balance between conveying unavoidable ambiguity and helping people and their family members find the best options for them.

- **Affect.** Physicians frequently miss opportunities to enter the emotional realm, which results in incomplete and unsatisfying conversations and personal and family failure to process information. Attention to feelings is key to successful planning and decision-making conversations. Clinicians must pay attention to their own feelings, too: a professional who is uncomfortable hearing people openly confront their illness can't hope to provide patients with realistic information about their prognosis or the support they need.

- **Hope.** Physicians "rightfully struggle to promote hope in the person with advanced disease and to support a positive outlook"—but hope may interfere with appropriate planning and behavior. The right mix may be for clinicians, people with advancing illness, and their families to "hope for the best but prepare for the worst."[26]

- **Communication among multiple providers.** Sharing medical information and coordinating care with the entire care team can be advanced by documenting discussions about family meetings and individual preferences in the medical record. We need electronic medical records that ease access to relevant progress notes, do-not-resuscitate (DNR) orders, POLST, and advance directives.[23,25]

Tulsky and other colleagues have developed and tested efficient interventions that markedly improve the communication skills of oncologists through multiday courses, as well as short Web-based interactive programs.

People with advancing illness and their families have a role in improving communication about treatment and care options, too, by knowing the right questions to ask and learning how to overcome difficulties in the system. The body of information about shared decision making and patient empowerment can help them with their side of the conversation.

Other innovations focus on media to communicate both the nature of a disease and the realities of medical interventions—the "medical facts" piece. One method that shows promise is using videos in addition to verbal descriptions to help patients define their goals of care and understand how they would be translated into medical care in the event of a life-threatening illness. Researchers saw positive results in preparing for the possibility of advanced dementia and are piloting the approach for people with advanced cancer or severe heart failure.[27,28]

Dedicated clinicians, researchers, ethicists, lawyers, and policy makers have helped us move the ball of advance care planning, but it will always be a challenging process to balance preparation with the need to act when the time comes. A nuanced view of planning focuses on preparing people and surrogates to participate with clinicians in "making the best possible in-the-moment decisions."[29] This preparation entails choosing an appropriate surrogate decision maker, clarifying and articulating the person's values and care preferences over time, and establishing leeway in surrogate decision making.

The central importance of person—and family—centered care

Chronic illness and disability affect the family as well as the individual. Health professionals must consider not only how the family caregiver can help the person with advancing illness or chronic disability but also how the provider must help the family.[30] In caring for people with serious and complex care needs, health professionals, social service providers, direct care workers (such as home care aides), the care recipient, and the family work as partners and members of the team to manage care and maintain quality of life.

In a person- and family-centered care model, family caregivers are no longer viewed as just a "resource" for their loved one; rather, they are partners and members of the care team. In this new paradigm, healthcare providers engage the individual and the family caregiver in informed advance care planning and shared decision making. Tools and information about treatment options are openly discussed and better communicated to clarify the person's and the family's values, beliefs, and goals of care. Advance care planning discussions may involve multiple conversations with the person and the family as the medical situation of the individual changes over time. Research has shown that the impact of such advance care planning can lessen emotional trauma, reduce depression, and diminish regret in surviving family members following the death of a loved one.[31,32]

It is also important—in a person- and family-centered approach—for the care team to recognize, assess, and address the direct support needs of family caregivers, including the awareness of the diversity of modern families. In order to cope better, family caregivers may themselves need information, skills training, and practical and emotional support, in addition to the elements of advance care planning. Because the focus of care is primarily on the individual, family caregivers may be reluctant to express their own needs and wishes, even though the needs of the family may exceed those of the person with advanced illness.[33] A key concern is that the continued reliance on family caregivers, without better recognition of their own support needs, could negatively affect the ability of family caregivers to provide care in the future.

A review of service interventions specifically for caregivers of cancer patients found significant positive effects on multiple outcomes. Caregivers experienced significantly less burden and fewer informational needs, increased ability to cope, and improved quality of life, including better physical health.[34] These interventions, like multicomponent interventions targeting dementia caregivers, who often experience the most demanding caregiving situations, appear to produce more informed, better prepared, and less strained caregivers. These positive outcomes, in turn, are likely to benefit the lives of persons with serious and advanced illness.

Caring for a relative or close friend with dementia is particularly stressful. Persons with dementia may have a prolonged period of gradual decline. Involving a person with dementia in decision making earlier and more actively than in the past can be beneficial for both the person and the family. Research has shown that persons with mild to moderate dementia are able to answer questions about their preferences for daily care and to choose a person to make decisions on their behalf.[35]

Family caregivers frequently experience the fragmentation within the healthcare system that is not set up to meet their needs or those of their loved ones, especially those who are sickest and most vulnerable. Large numbers of older adults with multiple chronic health conditions report duplicate tests and procedures, conflicting diagnoses for the same symptoms, contradictory medical information, and not receiving adequate information about potential drug interactions when they fill prescriptions.[36]

The lack of care coordination and communication across the healthcare and long-term care systems is a major concern of caregiving families.[37] When asked, many family caregivers say they want affordable, coordinated continuity of care and support for the practical and emotional needs of both the persons with advanced illness and the caregivers across service providers and care settings. In a truly person- and family-centered delivery system, families will benefit from advance care planning, more recognition and better support, palliative care with a team-based approach, and well-coordinated care to meet their needs and those for whom they care.

For the many people who already lack decision-making capacity due to dementia, other long-standing diagnoses, or a sudden health event, family caregivers play a key role in developing advance care plans and, often, in making decisions on behalf of the persons once capacity has diminished. Many caregivers who serve as proxy decision makers feel unprepared to do so and can benefit from guidance and support. The American Bar Association's proxy guide, *Making Medical Decisions for Someone Else: A How-To Guide*,[38] is one example of a practical tool to assist caregivers who serve as decision makers, and it has been replicated with state-specific information in at least five states. Healthcare providers need to recognize, though, that support for surrogate decision makers is not a one-stop shop but, rather, a long-term process, just as advance care planning is an evolving, iterative endeavor.

Getting There: Advancing Public Policy

How can we improve public discourse around the issues of advanced illness and advance care planning? We know from public opinion research that people believe these issues should be part of our national dialogue and that Medicare and other programs should support improved advanced illness care, palliative care, and access to information to enable informed choices and planning. People who have experienced the trauma of care that violated the individual patient's preferences and expressed wishes have spoken out and proposed policy and practice measures that will enhance person- and family-centered advanced illness care.

Just a few years ago, the Senate Special Committee on Aging held a hearing on "Honoring Final Wishes: How to Respect American's [sic] Choices at the End of Life." One senator spoke out about personal anguish when a grandmother who had previously expressed her wishes was intubated against her will and the "cloud" on the grieving of family members who suffered because they couldn't help their loved one. Another described his mother, who spent 12 years dying of Alzheimer's disease, had advance directives, and had four children who agreed on what she wanted yet the hospital refused to release her based on the Hippocratic oath's directive to "do no harm." The senator's distress over the hospital's perverse interpretation of this age-old ethic was palpable. These senators then developed proposed legislation to enhance advance care planning and care for serious illness. Yet today, after an innocuous provision in the health reform bill caused the "death panels" furor, even advocates for better advanced illness care agree that the term "end of life" is taboo in public. Individual and family needs are getting lost in the process.

In the current climate, Americans are confused and concerned. They know that advanced illness care options are important to them. They worry that they won't be told about their medical options and that they won't have control over the type of care they receive. Episodes of hospital-based care leave family caregivers wondering, "Who is caring for my loved one?" They don't really know what palliative care is. Almost a quarter of them believe, erroneously, that the health reform law allows a government panel to make end-of-life decisions for people on Medicare.

We need an honest and open public discussion of how best to support the needs, as well as the wishes, of those who are seriously ill and frail. We need to remind policy makers and the public that the goal is for American families and healthcare providers to collaborate in honoring people's preferences through a person- and family-centered care system. These preferences are about living their lives for as long as life remains. As geriatrician Mark Lachs put it, "The question is not if or even when but, really, 'how.' My goal for patients is that when they leave the planet . . . they do so enjoying the things they love most—family, golf, painting, theater, sex—ideally up until the very last minute possible."[39]

Naomi Karp, JD, is senior strategic policy advisor at the AARP Public Policy Institute. Karp has more than 30 years' experience in law and aging both as a frontline public interest lawyer and a Washington-based policy expert. Over the past 23 years she has focused her research and policy development on advance planning for healthcare and finances, elder abuse, guardianship, other fiduciary arrangements, and long-term care. At AARP, Karp completed a national study of the Physician Orders for Life-Sustaining Treatment (POLST) protocol, *Improving Advanced Illness Care: The Evolution of State POLST Programs.* She advises the AARP National Policy Council, government affairs staff, and other entities on advance care planning, end-of-life care, and patients' rights, as well as other topics within her areas of expertise. Previous publications include reports on healthcare decision making for the "unbefriended" elderly, diminished capacity and Medicare managed care, dispute resolution in healthcare, and a variety of reports involving legal protections for vulnerable older adults. Currently, Karp serves on the National Quality Forum Palliative and End-of-Life Steering Committee, reviewing quality measures in this arena. She serves on numerous national, regional, and local advisory groups, task forces, and coalitions; has written extensively for professional organizations and journals; and has a depth of experience in working with administrative agencies, legislatures, philanthropies, and the media. From 1988 to 2005, she served on the staff of the American Bar Association Commission on Law and Aging and previously was a legal services attorney representing low-income and older clients. She received her BA with honors from the University of Michigan and her law degree from Northeastern University.

Lynn Friss Feinberg, MSW, is a senior strategic policy advisor at the AARP Public Policy Institute, working on family caregiving and long-term care issues. Ms. Feinberg came to AARP from the National Partnership for Women and Families, serving as the first director of the Campaign for Better Care, an initiative to improve care in the United States for vulnerable older adults with multiple chronic conditions and their families. Previously, Ms. Feinberg served as deputy director of the National Center on Caregiving at the San Francisco–based Family Caregiver Alliance (FCA), where she was a leader in family-centered care for older adults, with special expertise in developing and replicating family caregiver support programs and translating research to promote policy change. During her more than two-decade tenure at FCA, she directed the National Consensus Project for Caregiver Assessment and led the first 50-state study on publicly funded caregiving programs in the United States. In 2007–2008, Ms. Feinberg was selected as the John Heinz Senate Fellow in Aging, serving in the office of U.S. Senator Barbara Boxer. She has published and lectured widely on family care issues and has served on numerous advisory boards and committees to address caregiving and long-term care issues. Ms. Feinberg is currently on the American Society of Aging's *Generations* editorial board, a commissioner of the American Bar Association's Commission on Law and Aging, a fellow of the Gerontological Society of America, and an elected member of the National Academy for Social Insurance. In 2006 she received the American Society on Aging's Leadership Award. Ms. Feinberg holds a master's degree in social welfare and gerontology from the University of California at Berkeley.

References

1. Gross J. *A bittersweet season: caring for our aging parents—and ourselves*. New York: Knopf; 2011.

2. Gawande A. Letting go: what should medicine do when it can't save your life? *The New Yorker*, August 2, 2010.

3. Living well at the end of life: a national conversation. *National Journal* Web site. http://syndication.nationaljournal.com/communications/ NationalJournalRegenceToplines.pdf. Accessed October 15, 2011.

4. Dinger E. AARP Massachusetts End of Life Survey. August 2005. http://www. mass.gov/Ihqcc/ docs/expert_panel/AARP_End_of_Life_Report%20Final.pdf. Accessed August 26, 2011.

5. Center to Advance Palliative Care. 2011 public opinion research on palliative care: a report based on research by public opinion strategies. http://www.capc. org/tools-for-palliative-care-programs/marketing/public-opinion-research/2011-public-opinion-research-on-palliative-care.pdf. Accessed August 26, 2011.

6. Nelson DV. AARP bulletin poll "getting ready to go" executive summary. January 2008. http://assets.aarp.org/rgcenter/il/getting_ready.pdf. Accessed August 26, 2011.

7. Perkins HS. Controlling death: the false promise of advance directives. *Annals of Internal Medicine*. 2007;147(1):51-57.

8. Kwak J, Haley WE. Current research findings on end-of-life decision making among racially or ethnically diverse groups. *Gerontologist*. 2005;45(5):634-641.

9. Thomson Reuters. National survey of healthcare consumers: end-of-life care. July 2010. http://www.factsforhealthcare.com/pressroom/NPR_report_ EndofLifeCare0710.pdf. Accessed August 26, 2011.

10. Keenan TA. Planning for long-term care: a survey of midlife and older women. October 2010. http://assets.aarp.org/rgcenter/general/ltc-planning-women.pdf. Accessed August 26, 2011.

11. Sulmasy DP, Snyder L. Substituted interests and best judgments: an integrated model of surrogate decision making. *JAMA: Journal of the American Medical Association*. 2010;304(17):1946-1947.

12. Whitlatch CJ, Feinberg LF. Family care and decision making. In: *Dementia and social work practice: research and interventions*. New York: Springer; 2007:129-148.

13. Pew Research Center. *Social and demographic trends: the decline of marriage and rise of new families.* November 10, 2010. http://pewsocialtrends.org/2010/11/18/the-decline-of-marriage-and-rise-of-new-families/. Accessed August 26, 2011.

14. Kane RL, Ouellette J. *The good caregiver: a one-of-a-kind compassionate resource for anyone caring for an aging loved one.* New York: Avery; 2011.

15. Feinberg L, Reinhard SC, Houser A, Choula R. Valuing the invaluable: 2011 update, the growing contributions and costs of family caregiving. June 2011. http://assets.aarp.org/rgcenter/ppi/ltc/i51-caregiving.pdf. Accessed August 26, 2011.

16. Rhee Y, Degenholtz HB, Lo Sasso AT, Emanuel LL. Estimating the quantity and economic value of family caregiving for community-dwelling older persons in the last year of life. *Journal of the American Geriatrics Society.* 2009;57(9):1654-1659.

17. Parker K. End-of-life decisions: how Americans cope. August 20, 2009. http://pewsocialtrends.org/2009/08/20/end-of-life-decisions-how-americans-cope/. Accessed August 26, 2011.

18. Roberto KA. Making critical health care decisions for older adults: consensus among family members. *Family Relations.* 1999;48(2):167-175.

19. Pew Research Center. Growing old in America: expectations vs. reality. August 20, 2009. http://pewsocialtrends.org/files/2010/10/Getting-Old-in-America.pdf. Accessed August 26, 2011.

20. Vig EK, Starks H, Taylor JS, Hopley EK, Fryer-Edwards K. Surviving surrogate decision-making: what helps and hampers the experience of making medical decisions for others. *Journal of General Internal Medicine.* 2007;22(9):1274-1279.

21. Gillick M. When lawyers practice medicine. *Perspectives on aging: a discussion of topical issues for baby boomers and their aging parents.* January 4, 2010. http://blog.drmurielgillick.com/2010/01/when-lawyers-practice-medicine.html. Accessed August 29, 2011.

22. Temel JS, Greer JA, Muzikansky A, et al. Early palliative care for patients with metastatic non-small-cell lung cancer. *New England Journal of Medicine.* 2010;363(8):733-742.

23. Sabatino CP, Karp N. Improving advanced illness care: the evolution of state POLST programs. http://assets.aarp.org/rgcenter/ppi/cons-prot/POLST-Report-04-11.pdf. Accessed October 19, 2011.

24. Hickman SE, Nelson CA, Perrin NA, Moss AH, Hammes BJ, Tolle SW. A comparison of methods to communicate treatment preferences in nursing facilities: traditional practices versus the physician orders for life-sustaining treatment program. *Journal of the American Geriatrics Society.* 2010;58(7):1241-1248.

25. Tulsky JA. Beyond advance directives: importance of communication skills at the end of life. *JAMA: Journal of the American Medical Association.* 2005;294(3):359-365.

26. Back AL, Arnold RM, Quill TE. Hope for the best, and prepare for the worst. *Annals of Internal Medicine.* 2003;138(5):439-443.

27. Volandes AE, Paasche-Orlow MK, Barry MJ, et al. Video decision support tool for advance care planning in dementia: randomised controlled trial. *BMJ.* 2009;338:b2159.

28. Gillick MR. Reversing the code status of advance directives? *New England Journal of Medicine.* 2010;362(13):1239-1240.

29. Sudore RL, Fried TR. Redefining the "planning" in advance care planning: preparing for end-of-life decision making. *Annals of Internal Medicine.* 2010;153(4):256-261.

30. Goetschius SK. Caring for families: the other patient in palliative care. In: Matzo ML, Sherman DW, eds. *Palliative care nursing: quality care to the end of life.* 3rd ed. New York: Springer; 2001:245-274.

31. Detering KM, Hancock AD, Reade MC, Silvester W. The impact of advance care planning on end of life care in elderly patients: randomised controlled trial. *BMJ.* 2010;340:c1345.

32. Wright AA, Zhang B, Ray A, et al. Associations between end-of-life discussions, patient mental health, medical care near death, and caregiver bereavement adjustment. *JAMA: Journal of the American Medical Association.* 2008;300(14):1665-1673.

33. Payne S, Hudson P. Assessing the family and caregivers. In: Walsh TD, Caraceni AT, Fainsinger R, et al, eds. *Palliative medicine.* Philadelphia: Saunders; 2008.

34. Northouse LL, Katapodi MC, Song L, Zhang L, Mood DW. Interventions with family caregivers of cancer patients: meta-analysis of randomized trials. *CA: A Cancer Journal for Clinicians.* 2010;60(5):317-339.

35. Feinberg LF, Whitlatch CJ. Decision-making for persons with cognitive impairment and their family caregivers. *American Journal of Alzheimer's Disease and Other Dementias.* 2002;17(4):237-244.

36. Anderson G. *Chartbook, chronic conditions: making the case for ongoing care.* Princeton, NJ: Robert Wood Johnson Foundation; 2007.

37. Feinberg L. A better way to care. *Aging Today.* May-June 2010:7.

38. American Bar Association Commission on Law and Aging. *Making medical decisions for someone else: a how-to guide.* Washington, DC: American Bar Association; 2009.

39. Lachs M. *Treat me, not my age: a doctor's guide to getting the best care as you or a loved one gets older.* New York: Viking; 2010.

Section IV

Where's the Money?

WE ALL KNOW that the cost of healthcare is high and rising rapidly. As patients, many of us fear both not being able to pay for these health services and being denied access to services that could help manage or treat us when we have serious illness. Of all American families that face advanced illness of a loved one, one-quarter faces bankruptcy because of healthcare expenses. The rapidly rising cost of healthcare is both personal and serious.

Could we redesign our healthcare delivery so that it both better addresses our healthcare needs when we have advanced illness AND controls the cost of healthcare? Achieving this twin goal would help us all.

It is easy to be skeptical that this two-part goal can be achieved. After all, when people have advanced illness, they need many medical services (e.g., hospitalizations, tests, physician care, drugs). It can appear that the only way to cut costs is to either voluntarily give up medical care or have it denied to you.

The underlying assumption behind this skepticism is that all the health services used by patients with advanced illness actually help them live longer and/or live better. The growing evidence is that many of the health services used when treating patients with advance illness do not improve things for the patient and, in fact, in many cases, may shorten life and unnecessarily increase suffering. This reality is what the authors in sections I and II were addressing with their innovative programs. There is a way to reorganize health services specifically for patients with advanced illness that not only improves things for the patient and his or her family but also helps lower cost by better management of the illness.

Besides the reports from sections I and II of this book, what other evidence do we have that we may overuse health services for patients with advanced illness and that by redesigning the delivery system we might not only lower the costs but also make things better for patients and their families?

In section IV, we have three articles that explore the problem of overutilization of health services for those patients with advanced illness. In chapter 13, William Brinson Weeks, MD, MBA, medical director for the Office of Professional Education and Outreach at the Dartmouth Institute for Health Policy and Clinical Practice, reviews the study of geographic variation of medical care in the last two years of life in the United States. As it turns out, some parts of the country use far more health services than other places, but all have similar outcomes. In chapter 14, Kyla R. Lee, MD, FACP, an internal medicine physician with a specialty in palliative medicine at Gundersen Health System, presents her single-institution report about how a hospital palliative care service both led to higher patient and family satisfaction with care and used less services—this at an institution where advance care planning is already very prevalent. Finally, in the closing chapter of this section, Diane Meier, MD, director of the Center to Advance Palliative Care, and R. Sean Morrison, MD, director of the National Palliative Care Research Center, build on their chapter 6 and describe how a palliative care approach benefits patients but changes what and how healthcare services are used. There is strong evidence that this approach helps control the overall cost of care.

In healthcare in the United States, both healthcare institutions and the news media love to tell stories of new technological breakthroughs and medical miracles. Perhaps the accounts in this book need to be put into the same story line. Here we have identified an unexpected but important new "breakthrough" in medicine. This breakthrough is not a new drug or test or treatment; it is a new way to organize our care of patients with advance illness so that they live as well as possible for as long as possible in the way of their own choosing. The "miracle" is that this new care depends more on human interaction and coordination than on technology and science. The wonder is that it costs less to deliver but is actually better.

thirteen

Variation in Health Services Utilization at the End of Life: A Summary of the Evidence

—William Brinson Weeks, MD, MBA

IN A LANDMARK 1973 *Science* article, Wennberg and Gittelsohn reported dramatic variation in health services utilization across healthcare service areas in Vermont.[1] When comparing population-based measures across 13 hospital service areas, they found that patients living in the service areas with the highest use experienced two to three times more utilization, bed supply, manpower, and expenditures than those living in service areas with the lowest use. Population-based rates of specific surgical procedures varied even more across service areas—12-fold for tonsillectomy and 7-fold for varicose vein stripping—and were correlated with the availability of surgical specialists providing these services. Their conclusion was counterintuitive to the conventional wisdom at the time: "Given the magnitude of these variations, the possibility of too much medical care and the attendant likelihood of iatrogenic illness is presumably as strong as the possibility of not enough service and unattended morbidity and mortality."[1]

Since then, focusing on the Medicare fee-for-service population, researchers at the Dartmouth Institute for Health Policy and Clinical Practice have continued to examine variation in health services utilization. While they have consistently demonstrated widespread variation in health services utilization, more recently they turned their attention to examining what services higher health expenditures purchased and whether those expenditures resulted in improved technical quality of care, patient satisfaction, or health outcomes for patients.[2,3] After providing a brief overview of how the research is conducted, this chapter will summarize the key findings of that work.

How the Research Is Conducted

Why Medicare data are used

The ability to interpret research on health services utilization is predicated on having complete information as to where patients obtain care and the types of care they get. There are several ways that one can elicit such information. One can directly ask patients. However, this method depends on getting a good response rate from patients; it assumes that recall of health services used—usually asked with respect to use over the past six months or year—is accurate and comparable to how other patients might report use, and it might miss the sickest patients, those who die after enrollment, those who become too sick to respond to the survey, and those who are hospitalized when the survey follow-up takes place.

Another method of obtaining health services utilization data is to ask healthcare systems for data on their patients. The challenge with this method is that while a healthcare system has information on the services that patients use within its own system, it does not have access to information on care provided outside the system. In addition, because many healthcare systems contract with providers instead of employ them, they may not consistently collect health services utilization even on patients who use health system affiliates.

On the other hand, insurers collect comprehensive information on health services utilization because they bill for and reimburse them. The problem with this source of data is that the proportion of patients covered by a particular insurer varies considerably across markets. Therefore, the ability to make comparisons across regions is limited. Further, because privately insured patients can change insurance companies, the ability to track patients' utilization across time can be difficult.

Established in 1965 and administered by the federal government, Medicare is a social insurance program designed to provide a portion of the healthcare costs of patients who have paid a payroll tax for a minimum of 10 nonconsecutive years and who are either disabled or have reached age 65. Currently, that payroll tax is 2.9% of income; in 2013, the tax will increase to 3.8% for individuals making more than $200,000 per year. Medicare was designed as a "pay-as-you-go" program, wherein those currently paying the payroll taxes would pay for those who were eligible at the time and thereby develop neither surpluses nor deficits. However, because of longer life spans, the baby boom population, and high medical inflation, Medicare is now anticipating substantial deficits in the future; in 2009, the "unfunded liability" for Medicare was approximately $36 trillion, or about 2.5 times the U.S. gross domestic product that year.

Patients who have contributed to Medicare through payroll tax deductions for 10 quarters are automatically covered by Medicare Part A, which pays for inpatient hospital care, inpatient care in skilled nursing facilities, hospice care, and home healthcare services. Patients who are enrolled in Medicare Part A can pay a monthly premium to enroll in Medicare Part B, which pays for medically necessary services such as doctors' services obtained during hospitalization and outpatient care. Using Medicare data to evaluate health services utilization has the following advantages:

- Consistently reported national data are available. Medicare reimbursement policies and billing codes are consistent across the United States, allowing data on health services utilization from different geographic areas to be compared.

• Because the number and characteristics of Medicare beneficiaries are known, age-, sex-, and race-adjusted population-based rates can be calculated. This allows for fair comparisons of service utilization across geographic areas.

• Patients who enroll in Medicare tend to stay enrolled. This allows researchers to track patients over time, regardless of whether they move, change healthcare providers, or change healthcare systems.

• Medicare spending represents a substantial proportion of healthcare expenditures in the United States, and it is anticipated to grow. Therefore, examination of policy ramifications associated with changes in healthcare utilization patterns in this population is important and meaningful.

How the data are aggregated

First, data are limited to patients who are concurrently enrolled in both Medicare Part A and Medicare Part B for the entire year being examined. This is because Dartmouth Atlas researchers want to understand both hospital-based and physician-based health services utilization. Also, analyses are limited to patients who are Medicare eligible by virtue of age; patients who are eligible because of disability or need for dialysis are excluded. This is done because researchers believe that disabled patients and those requiring dialysis are sufficiently different from the overall Medicare-eligible population that their exclusion is warranted.

Medicare billing data include information on the patient, including ZIP code of residence and the place where the patient obtained care. Data on service utilization are first examined at the patient ZIP code level. Each ZIP code is aggregated to one of approximately 3,300 hospital service areas based on where patients in that ZIP code obtain the plurality of their care. For instance, should Medicare beneficiaries in one ZIP code obtain 40% of their care at hospital A, 30% at hospital B, and 30% at hospital C, all care for Medicare beneficiaries in that ZIP code will be allocated to hospital A.

In a similar fashion, hospital service area data are aggregated to 306 hospital referral regions across the nation, based on where patients in the hospital service areas obtain the plurality of their tertiary care, such as cardiac surgery and neurosurgery. Aggregation to hospital referral regions both reduces the variation in services utilization seen at the hospital service area, making utilization measures more stable over time, and allows for examination of variation of geographic data that are collected irregularly or on only a sample of Medicare beneficiaries, such as data on patient satisfaction or data that are obtained from other sources, such as information on the physician service population.

Finally, to make comparisons on service utilization counts meaningful, counts of care are converted to dollars, using standardized prices. This eliminates differences in true costs of care that are due to differences in Medicare reimbursement caused by variation in regional labor costs and differences in teaching hospital status.

Limitations of the methodology

There are several limitations to using Medicare data. First, while we believe that resource utilization among Medicare beneficiaries is likely to reflect utilization patterns among non-Medicare beneficiaries, the degree to which that is true is unknown. Second, the Medicare-eligible population examined is older and sicker than the non-Medicare-eligible population. Thus, their experiences in the healthcare system may not reflect those of the non-Medicare-eligible population. Third, patients who are insured through employee benefits, by the Veterans Administration system, or by some other mechanism are not included in the sample.

Key Research Findings

Over the past two decades of research, a persistent finding has been that Medicare spending varies dramatically across hospital referral regions in the United States. In 2007, overall inflation-adjusted rates of reimbursement for noncapitated Medicare per enrollee varied more than threefold—from $5,221 in the Honolulu, Hawaii, hospital referral region to $17,274 in the Salem, Oregon, hospital referral region (http://www.dartmouthatlas.org). These patterns are consistent over time and appear to reflect stable, geographically defined patterns of diagnostic intensity. Not only do high-cost and high-utilization areas tend to remain high cost and high utilization over time but also patients who move from low-care-delivery-intensity regions to high-care-delivery-intensity regions become more intensively diagnosed in their new homes, while those moving from high- to low-intensity regions become less intensively diagnosed.[4]

A second finding is that rates of growth in spending vary dramatically across hospital referral regions. The annual growth rate in per capita total Medicare inflation-adjusted expenditures varied more than fivefold from 1.63% in the Honolulu, Hawaii, hospital referral region to 8.31% in the McAllister, Texas, hospital referral region. Because high-cost hospital referral regions also have higher healthcare cost growth rates, reducing the rates of growth in spending among high-growth spending areas could lead to substantial reductions in healthcare costs. For instance, reducing annual growth in per capita spending from 3.5% (the national average) to 2.4% (the rate in San Francisco) would leave Medicare with an estimated balance of $758 billion by 2023, as opposed to a deficit of $660 billion, thereby creating a cumulative savings of $1.42 trillion over a 15-year period.[5]

Importantly, research from the Dartmouth Atlas Project has demonstrated that greater utilization is not associated with better outcomes. The project has classified healthcare services into three categories: evidence-based care, which measures clinical application of medical interventions that have been shown to work, such as administration of aspirin after heart attack; patient preference–sensitive care, that is, the types of care wherein patients with different value systems might reasonably choose different treatments, such as watchful waiting versus prostatectomy for benign prostatic hypertrophy; and supply-sensitive care, wherein the supply of resources governs their use. Among cohorts of patients with the same diagnoses, higher spending does not buy more evidence-based care or patient preference–sensitive care; however, higher spending does buy more supply-sensitive medical services, such as physician visits, hospital bed days of care, laboratory tests, and radiology examinations. With respect to patient outcomes among these same cohorts of patients, risk-adjusted mortality rates were actually higher in high-cost regions.[6] Higher spending also does not result in better quality of care, regardless of whether one examines the technical quality of hospital[7] or ambulatory[8] care. Finally, higher spending is not associated with patient perceptions of the accessibility or quality of medical care[9] or their hospital experiences.[10]

Care at the end of life

Dartmouth Atlas Project researchers have completed a number of studies that examine care at the end of life. To examine this aspect of care, researchers identify Medicare beneficiaries who have died and retrospectively examine their health services utilization in the two years preceding death. Numerous studies have found that care at the end of life is expensive and shows dramatic variation in costs, much of which appear to be wasteful. In the last two years of their lives, patients with chronic illness account for about a third of Medicare spending, much of it going toward physician and hospital fees associated with repeat hospitalizations (http://www.dartmouth atlas.org/keyissues/issue.aspx?con=2944). Even when only highly regarded medical centers were examined, striking variation was found in the care patients received in the last six months of their lives: the number of days in hospital per decedent ranged from 9.4 to 27, the number of days in intensive care units ranged from 1.6 to 9.5, the number of physician visits ranged from 17.6 to 76.2, the percentage of patients seeing 10 or more physicians ranged from 16.9% to 58.5%, hospice enrollment ranged from 10.8% to 43.8%, the percentage of deaths occurring in hospital ranged from 15.9% to 55.6%, and the percentage of deaths associated with a stay in intensive care ranged from 8.4% to 36.8%.[11] Among Medicare beneficiaries over age 65 years with poor-prognosis cancers, care at the end of life varies markedly across regions: more than a third of these patients spent their last days in hospitals and in intensive care units; use of hospice varied markedly; and, in some hospitals, referral to hospice occurred so close to the date of death that it was unlikely to have served its purpose of providing assistance and comfort to patients and their families.[12]

Interpreting variation and what to do about it

Variation in healthcare services utilization is seen wherever researchers look, both in the United States and internationally. Variation can be divided into two categories: variation that is warranted and due to differences in the health, healthcare needs, or healthcare desires of the population and variation that is unwarranted or due simply to differences in the supply of service providers.

There are several ways to reduce unwarranted variation. First, expanding the concept of informed consent to "informed choice" by objectively outlining choices that patients have to address their medical conditions, including the choice of obtaining palliative care at the end of life, can reduce unwarranted variation. For the informed choice process to work, impartial, accurate, and pertinent information about choices and local care patterns must be made available to patients. Research suggests that implementation of an informed choice process will help reduce waste, dissatisfaction with care, and unwarranted variation in health services utilization at the end of life.[13] Importantly, shared goals that involve the input of the patient, family members, and the care team—and that address outcomes such as pain control, dignity, and quality of life—must be formulated. Information that is conveyed to patients should be in a form that allows them to accurately assess the impact of an intervention on their health or prognosis. Absolute risks are critical aspects of accurate information, and communication devices such as a "drug facts" box[14] or diagnosis-specific decision aids[13,15,16] can help transform the informed consent process to one of "informed choice."

Second, while the Medicare payroll tax is distributed equally among workers in the United States, it is consumed quite differently from place to place. Helping taxpayers understand this may reduce unwarranted variation. Among Medicare beneficiaries who died between 2001 and 2005, total age-, sex-, race-, and chronic condition–adjusted Medicare costs for the two years prior to death varied almost threefold, from $29,111 in Dubuque, Iowa, to $81,143 in Manhattan, New York, while the national average for such spending was $43,879 (Figure 1).

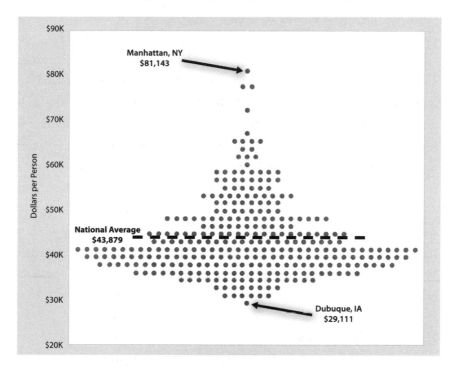

Taxpayers who live in hospital referral regions that spend below the national average are paying not only for their own Medicare services but also for a portion of those for patients who live in hospital referral regions that spend above the national average; at the extreme, Dubuque residents are subsidizing Manhattan residents' Medicare expenditures. That those bearing a disproportionate share of the spending costs are not compensated in another form—whether through reimbursement or increased representation—fundamentally constitutes taxation without representation. Unless efforts to reduce any Medicare deficits are pro-portionally allocated to geographic regions according to their historic spending pattern, the problem will perpetuate and, given the different spending growth rates, compound into the indefinite future.

The issue of variation in spending at the end of life will ultimately have to be reconciled through spending constraints in the higher-cost regions, additional regional Medicare taxes, or a combination of the two. If clinical practice patterns result in overuse of medical interventions but do not produce better clinical outcomes, patient satisfaction, or patient perception of increased access to care, then value, which is defined as quality divided by cost, has been reduced: the denominator has risen while the numerator remains the same or, in some cases, has gone down. Similarly, should resources be allocated to medical interventions that do not improve outcomes, satisfaction, or other measures of quality while medical interventions that could have resulted in improved population health were not implemented because resources were scarce, those resources that were consumed constitute waste. Ironically, over time, the implementation of low-value and wasteful services indirectly leads to higher fiscal costs, because the waste now embedded in the system is passed on to patients in the form of higher co-payments and premiums, which patients receive in lieu of higher wages.

Conclusion

This chapter has summarized some of the research findings that demonstrate widespread variation in health service utilization and costs but do not demonstrate positive correlations with technical quality, patient satisfaction, or outcomes. These findings raise ethical questions about the appropriate distribution of scarce resources nationally, how such variation might adversely impact patients regionally, and the importance of informing patients about variation so that they can make informed decisions about healthcare locally. These findings can help move the country from discussions about "death panels" to discussions about appropriate use of scarce resources, with a focus on resources whose consumption does not improve the fate of patients and so can confidently be labeled waste; from discourse in which regions defend current healthcare utilization patterns as responses to unspecified patient needs to discourse about what patient needs are and how healthcare delivery systems can appropriately, efficiently, and effectively understand and meet those needs; and from conversations about "doing everything" to extend the length of a life without regard to its quality to conversations about how healthcare systems can make dying—the unavoidable sequel to living—comfortable, dignified, and humane.

⌘

William B. Weeks, MD, MBA, is a graduate of Whitman College (BS), the University of Texas Medical Branch (MD), and Columbia University (MBA). After practicing clinical psychiatry for five years, he pursued a career as a health services researcher within the VA system, where his work focused on variation in physician incomes; in the types, quality, and outcomes of health services that veterans obtained through the VA and through Medicare; and in the types and quantities of care needed and received by rural, as opposed to urban-dwelling, veterans. He received the National Rural Health Association's Rural Health Outstanding Researcher Award in 2009. Currently, he is associate professor and core faculty at the Dartmouth Institute for Health Policy and Clinical Practice, where he teaches, conducts health services research, and serves as medical director for TDI's Office of Professional Education and Outreach and as medical director of the High Value Healthcare Collaborative, a consortium of 14 healthcare systems across the nation that are committed to improving the value of the health services that they deliver.

References

1.   Wennberg J, Gittelsohn A. Small area variations in health care delivery. *Science.* 1973;182(117):1102-1108.

2.   Fisher ES, Goodman D, Skinner J, Bronner K. Health care spending, quality, and outcomes: more isn't always better. *Dartmouth Institute for Health Policy & Clinical Practice*. 2010. http://www.dartmouthatlas.org/downloads/reports/Spending_Brief_022709.pdf. Accessed September 14, 2011.

3.   Wennberg JE. *Tracking medicine: a researcher's quest to understand health care.* Oxford: Oxford University Press; 2010.

4.   Song Y, Skinner J, Bynum J, Sutherland J, Wennberg JE, Fisher ES. Regional variations in diagnostic practices. *New England Journal of Medicine*. 2010;363(1):45-53.

5.   Fisher ES, Bynum JP, Skinner JS. Slowing the growth of health care costs—lessons from regional variation. *New England Journal of Medicine*. 2009;360(9):849-852.

6.   Fisher ES, Wennberg DE, Stukel TA, Gottlieb DJ, Lucas FL, Pinder EL. The implications of regional variations in Medicare spending. Pt 1: the content, quality, and accessibility of care. *Annals of Internal Medicine*. 2003;138(4):273-287.

7.   Yasaitis L, Fisher ES, Skinner JS, Chandra A. Hospital quality and intensity of spending: is there an association? *Health Affairs (Millwood)*. 2009;28(4):w566-w572.

8.   Fisher ES, Wennberg DE, Stukel TA, Gottlieb DJ. Variations in the longitudinal efficiency of academic medical centers. *Health Affairs (Millwood)*. 2004;Suppl Variation:VAR19-32.

9.   Fowler FJ Jr, Gallagher PM, Anthony DL, Larsen K, Skinner JS. Relationship between regional per capita Medicare expenditures and patient perceptions of quality of care. *JAMA: Journal of the American Medical Association*. 2008;299(20):2406-2412.

10. Wennberg JE, Bronner K, Skinner JS, Fisher ES, Goodman DC. Inpatient care intensity and patients' ratings of their hospital experiences. *Health Affairs (Millwood)*. 2009;28(1):103-112.

11. Wennberg JE, Fisher ES, Stukel TA, Skinner JS, Sharp SM, Bronner KK. Use of hospitals, physician visits, and hospice care during last six months of life among cohorts loyal to highly respected hospitals in the United States. *B*. 2004;328(7440):607.

12. Goodman DC, Fisher ES, Chang C-H, et al. Quality of end-of-life cancer care for Medicare beneficiaries. Regional and hospital-specific analyses. *Dartmouth Institute for Health Policy & Clinical Practice*. 2010. http://www.dartmouthatlas.org/downloads/reports/Cancer_report_11_16_10.pdf. Accessed September 14, 2011.

13. O'Connor AM, Wennberg JE, Legare F, et al. Toward the 'tipping point': Decision aids and informed patient choice. *Health Affairs (Millwood)*. 2007;26(3):716-725.

14. Schwartz LM, Woloshin S, Welch HG. Using a drug facts box to communicate drug benefits and harms: two randomized trials. *Annals of Internal Medicine*. 2009;150(8):516-527.

15. Wennberg JE, Barry MJ, Fowler FJ, Mulley A. Outcomes research, PORTs, and health care reform. *Ann N Y Acad Sci*. 1993;703:52-62.

16. Welch HG. Informed choice in cancer screening. *JAMA: Journal of the American Medical Association*. 2001;285(21):2776-2778.

fourteen

"The Right Care, Right Here": How a Palliative Service Made Things Better for Patients

—*Kyla R. Lee, MD, FACP*

AFTER MEDICAL SCHOOL, I moved from New York to La Crosse, Wisconsin, to join a hospital not only known for its excellence in medical care but also recognized as a national leader in providing patient-centered care. I felt so strongly about the care at Gundersen Health System[1] that when my mother was found to have an ovarian mass, I flew her and my father from the heart of New York City to this Midwest hospital for care. A few years later in 2005, a team of internal medicine doctors, cancer doctors, and nurse practitioners collaborated to launch a new medical hospital service to help better manage the symptoms and conditions of patients with advanced illness (a palliative care service). With this additional team to focus on complex symptom control in advanced disease, we expanded our ability to fulfill the promise of Gundersen's motto, "the right care, right here."

This new hospital palliative service was built on a long tradition of services aimed at addressing the medical and social needs of patients with advanced illness, such as cancer, heart failure, and emphysema. Gundersen's hospice program had already been caring for patients in the last six months of life since 1980. Then, in 1993, Gundersen began offering palliative consults through a seasoned and compassionate nurse practitioner who collaborated with the hospice medical director to allow for inpatient hospital pain management consults and visits aimed at such issues as nausea control at chairside consults during chemotherapy. In addition, Gundersen Health System had a longstanding history of assisting almost all of our patients and their families with advance care planning. This meant that as a medical community, the treating team and family almost always knew what values and decisions our patients had clarified around their medical choices prior to an emergent event.

As an internal medicine physician, I recognized, however, that because I often oversaw the care of patients admitted to our hospital, amid a busy call night with 17 new admissions, there was minimal time in the hospital for the treating physician to sit and discuss in depth the individual goals and options with patients and their families. Patients these days come in more critically ill with multiple problems, including many with advanced diseases and a laundry list of medications. The challenge is that there are usually multiple interventions and tests—and the benefits and burdens of each—to consider. This is the point at which a dedicated palliative team could help patients and their families navigate the rough waters of changing health in a deeper and more personalized way. The dream of a true multidisciplinary team with the focus on symptom control and comfort care was allowed to blossom at our hospital with a committed group of six physicians, three nurse practitioners, social workers, hospital chaplains, and floor nurses with specialized training. The Gundersen leadership supported this service line because they knew that it aided our patient-centered model by allowing for the time and discussions needed by patients and their families when making these difficult decisions.

Unlike other facilities, our hospital had been working on advance care planning since the 1990s. Therefore, at our start in 2005, we already had effective advance care planning systems, and our patients almost always participated in planning. Through the numbers posted by Dartmouth Atlas, Gundersen leadership knew that our cost of care in the last two years of life was extremely low compared with that of other hospitals. If that was already happening at Gundersen Health System, could a palliative care team have any effect on the cost of care? Honestly, I was skeptical about whether the palliative team could improve on those outcomes since delivering the "right care" had already led to higher patient satisfaction and lower costs. The question remained: would the addition of a palliative care team make any statistically significant difference in outcomes and cost of care at Gundersen? Therefore, I decided to review our data to determine how the new hospital palliative service performed in this unique environment where care was already very patient centered and patients were making choices that limited unwanted medical interventions. Moreover, I wanted to study a group of patients who had an unpredictable course of advanced illness.

It has long been recognized that some disease pathways are easier to predict than others. For example, cancer patients often experience a sudden decline in which the body can no longer withstand the chemotherapy or the cancer advances despite all treatment. At this point it is clearer for patients, families, and doctors to predict the trajectory of decline over weeks to months until death. As palliative care extends into other advanced disease states, such as renal failure, congestive heart failure (CHF), or congestive obstructive pulmonary disease (COPD, including emphysema), it is more difficult to predict how the patient's course will go. Many times, not only are there medicines and treatments that can improve the quality of life but also the duration of decline is often far slower than in other diseases. After years of debilitating symptoms, relatively minor challenges to the body, such as infection, can lead to death.

Previously collected data from Gundersen showed that after a hospital stay, patients who had received care from the palliative service were significantly more satisfied with care than were other similar patients who had not received it. This was great news for the palliative team. But we wanted to know whether providing palliative care changed other aspects of care. Gundersen Health System is a

"Top 100" heart hospital with a specialized CHF clinic with an average of 1,000 admissions a year for treatment of CHF, so I chose to focus my study on these patients and their need for days in critical care units, hospice enrollments, and cost of care, as palliative care became a part of our already "efficient" hospital.

Methods

Our study was designed to compare the resources used by patients with CHF who received palliative care services (PCS) with those of CHF patients receiving usual care (non-PCS). The study was a retrospective, nonrandomized comparison of resource use that used data recorded in our billing systems for patients hospitalized between June 15, 2005, and June 15, 2006.

All consecutive hospital admissions between June 15, 2005, and June 15, 2006, at Gundersen Health system were queried in the electronic medical record for billing codes including CHF in the top three admission and discharge diagnoses. A total of 1,041 patients with possible CHF at admission were identified. Each of these 1,043 medical records was reviewed by a single physician to determine, through the admission note, discharge note, radiology records, and consult notes, whether the patient had been actively treated for CHF during the hospitalization. Each was read without the knowledge of their status of interaction with the palliative care team.

After clinical review, 430 patients who had not been actively treated for CHF were excluded from the study, leaving a total of 611 patients. These 611 patients were divided into two groups: patients with CHF without palliative care input (non-PCS; n = 504) and patients with CHF who had received input by the palliative care team by either consult or direct admission into the palliative care service (PCS; n = 107). In the PCS group (n = 107), a subgroup of patients (n = 64) had received a palliative consult prior to hospital admission, through either the palliative care clinic or a previous hospital consult. This subgroup of prior palliative care service patients (prior-PCS) was also evaluated for any significant trends.

The data were analyzed using t-tests and x^2 tests to determine the significance of the relationship between variables. A P value <.05 was considered significant.

Results

Demographic variables for the 107 PCS patients and 504 non-PCS patients are summarized in Table 1. The PCS group differed significantly from the non-PCS group, in that its patients were older on average, it had a higher proportion of women, its use of acute hospital resources was lower, and its referral rate to hospice was higher. There were no significant differences in ethnicity.

The average length of acute care days for PCS and non-PCS patients was the same, at an average of four days. PCS and non-PCS patient admissions to the hospital via the emergency department were similar (54% vs. 56%, respectively; P = .66). PCS patients had significantly lower average total hospital, radiology, and physician charges than did non-PCS patients. The PCS patients' average total laboratory and pharmacy charges were lower than those of the non-PCS patients, as well, but not significantly so.

As in previous studies with palliative care for patients with cancer, we found that patients with CHF in the PCS group were more likely to be readmitted within 31 days (P < .001) than were their non-PCS counterparts. When the greater average age of the PCS group was adjusted for by excluding patients under age 75 years, the difference in readmission rate was no longer significant (P < .08). As expected in the PCS group, which was older and had more medical problems, it had a higher rate of death per hospitalization (19% vs. 6%; P < .001). Compared with non-PCS patients, a significantly larger proportion of PCS patients surviving to discharge from the hospital were admitted to hospice (5% vs. 46%; P < .0001).

In the original 107 patients cared for by the Palliative Care Service, a subgroup of patients (n = 64) had received a palliative consult prior to the index hospital admission for CHF, through either the palliative care clinic or prior in-patient hospital consult (prior-PCS).

We compared the demographic and resource utilization data of these 64 prior-PCS patients with those of the 504 non-PCS patients (Table 2). Like the original PCS group, the prior-PCS group differed significantly from the non-PCS group, in that it was older on average, had a higher proportion of women, had a lower use of acute hospital resources, and had a higher referral rate to hospice.

In our study of patients with CHF admitted to the hospital, the average length of acute care days for prior-PCS and non-PCS patients was significantly different, at an average of three days versus four days ($P < .041$). There was no difference between the prior-PCS and the non-PCS patient admissions to the hospital via the emergency department (54% vs. 56%; $P < .708$). Prior-PCS patients were significantly less likely than the non-PCS patients to require the resources of the intensive care unit (27% vs. 52%; $P < .001$).

Prior-PCS patients were found to have significantly lower average total hospital, radiology, and physician charges than were the non-PCS patients. Moreover, prior-PCS patients' average total laboratory and pharmacy charges were now also significantly lower than those of the non-PCS patients ($P < .002$ and $P < .001$, respectively).

Unlike the initial palliative care group, we found that patients with CHF in the prior-PCS group had no difference in readmission rates when compared with the non-PCS group ($P < .079$). As expected, the prior-PCS group, which was older, had a higher rate of death per hospitalization (23% vs. 6%; $P < .001$). Of the original 613 patients, 69 patients elected a hospice program at discharge—40, an outpatient program, and 29, an inpatient program. Compared with non-PCS patients, a significantly larger proportion of the prior-PCS patients were admitted to hospice (5% vs. 41%; $P < .001$).

Table 1. Comparison of Non-PCS and PCS Patients by Age and Health Resource Utilization

Variable	Non-PCS n = 504	PCS n = 107	P value
Average age, years	73	80	.001
Length of stay, days	4	4	NS
Total hospital charges	$22,976	$15,944	.001
Total laboratory charges	$3,052	$2,435	NS
Total pharmacy charges	$2,579	$2,060	NS
Total radiology charges	$211	$166	.002
All physician consult and evaluation charges	$5,511	$3,279	.001
Intensive care unit admission	263 (52%)	42 (39%)	.015
Inpatient hospital mortality	32 (6%)	20 (18%)	.0001
Referral to outpatient or inpatient hospice	29 (.05%)	42 (38%)	.0001

NS = not significant.

TABLE 2. Comparison of Non-PCS Patients and PCS Plus Prior PCS Input Patients
(Prior-PCS)

Variable	Non-PCS $n = 504$	Prior-PCS $n = 64$	P value
Average age, years	73	82	.001
Length of stay, days	4	3	.041
Total hospital charges	$22,976	$11,895	.001
Total laboratory charges	$3,052	$1,759	.01
Total pharmacy charges	$2,579	$1,482	.002
Total radiology charges	$211	$104	.001
All physician consult and evaluation charges	$5,511	$2,562	.001
Inpatient hospital mortality, n (%)	32 (6%)	15 (23%)	.001
Intensive care unit, n (%)	263 (52%)	17 (26%)	.001

Conclusion

Even though Gundersen Health System has successfully implemented advance care planning and has low healthcare cost in the last two years of life, these data suggest that early initiation of a palliative care consult for advanced illness such as CHF provided a meaningful new service for patients and family who elected care that resulted in fewer ICU days and more referrals to programs such as hospice to help support quality at the end of life. Patients who had a discussion with a member of the palliative care team in either a clinic setting or a hospital setting prior to the acute hospitalization experienced these improvements, as well.

While identifying these data is important, it is not the data that are ultimately important; rather, it is the lives of our patients and their families that matter the most. Ultimately, it is the patient and family that drive the wish for humane and quality-of-life choices.

So, how does this new service matter to you and the patients we serve? Here's one story. Joseph had labored all his life as a carpenter raising the large Catholic family that had gathered around his hospital bedside. In his hospital room it was loud, and there was much visiting despite his waning energy. Joe has spent four years following the guidelines of CHF clinic, allowing him this extra time. The day he was admitted to the hospital, his heart no longer pumped effectively, and he was so weak he had to roll out of the bathtub to finally call for help. His children surrounded him, and, interestingly, his son had chosen to be a surgeon and his daughter an intensive care nurse, so there were powerful insights into the complexity of medical decision making. Joe knew inside that his time was short. He had maximized his medical therapy, and the adjustment overnight had not improved his situation. After discussion with the palliative care team, he and his family elected to stay at Gundersen in the inpatient hospice program. In those four remaining days, the visiting, the family stories, and the heartfelt conversations framed his good-bye. My work as his doctor was to carefully control his symptoms and give him the best family time possible. This was the "right care, right here" for Joe and his family.

Kyla R. Lee, MD, FACP, is a founding member of the Palliative Care Hospitalist Team at Gundersen Health System. Dr. Lee has more than 12 years of experience in internal medicine and hospice care. She is board certified in internal medicine (2003) and has specialty board certification in hospice and palliative care (2008). She did intensive training and refocused her research to include palliative care during her time at the Harvard University Program in Palliative Care Education and Practice in 2006. Dr. Lee is active in clinical practice, research, and education. She works as an internal medicine physician and is director of the Internal Medicine Clerkship, as well as serving as a hospitalist on the Palliative and Hospice Care Team. She received her BS from the University of Vermont, her master's in education/counseling psychology at Harvard University, and her MD from the University of Wisconsin School of Medicine and Public Health.

Reference

1. Gundersen Health System is a physician-led, not-for-profit, tertiary referral center located in western Wisconsin. Gundersen Health System is a comprehensive healthcare network serving a 19-county area of central Wisconsin, southeastern Minnesota, and northwestern Iowa. The system has one of the nation's largest multispecialty group medical practices and serves as the western campus for the University of Wisconsin School of Medicine and Public Health.

fifteen

Better Care, Higher Quality, and Lower Costs for the Seriously Ill

—Diane E. Meier, MD,
and R. Sean Morrison, MD

PERHAPS THE SINGLE biggest threat to economic recovery in the United States is spiraling healthcare costs. In 2009, spending on healthcare approached 18% of the U.S. gross domestic product (GDP) and has consistently grown faster than the economy overall since the 1960s.[1] Centers for Medicare and Medicaid Services (CMS) project that by 2018, healthcare spending will be more than $4.3 trillion, or $13,100 per resident, and will account for 20.3% of GDP.[1] While discussions about the costs of healthcare often focus on the average amount spent per person, spending on health services is actually quite skewed.[1] Less than 10% of Medicare expenditures account for 63% of healthcare spending, and the sickest 1% of the population (the most seriously ill) drive 21% of healthcare expenditures.[1] Conversely, the "worried well," that is, the 50% of the population with average healthcare needs (prevention, acute episodic illness, minor injury) account for just 3% of spending.[1] As described in chapter 6, palliative care programs targeting the sickest and most costly patient populations have been shown to improve clinical quality, enhance patient and family satisfaction, and promote patient-centered care. In this chapter, we describe how palliative care teams can both improve value in healthcare and reduce costs. We additionally address steps that need to be undertaken in order to ensure the ongoing delivery of high-quality palliative care.

Palliative Care Improves Value in Healthcare

Value in healthcare has been defined as the ratio of quality to cost. Value can be enhanced by improving quality (chap. 6), by reducing cost, or—preferably, as in the case of palliative care—both. Data from the Dartmouth Atlas of Health Care and others[2,3] suggest that the key contributors of healthcare costs in the setting of serious illness include increased utilization of hospitals, specialists, and costly diagnostic tests and procedures. In the long term, reducing the denominator of the value equation will require multifaceted interventions that address the financial incentives favoring treatment quantity and care fragmentation, lack of training in management of patients with complex or multiple chronic conditions, absence of a strong primary care infrastructure that truly coordinates care and ensures appropriate access and referrals to organ-specific specialists, and financial and structural fragmentation that exists between acute and postacute healthcare settings.

At present, however, only one intervention has been shown empirically to directly enhance the value equation: palliative care. By addressing pain and symptoms that might otherwise increase hospital complications and lengths of stay, meeting with patients and families to establish clear care goals, tailoring treatments to those goals in consultation with the patients and their families, and developing comprehensive safe discharge plans, palliative care teams ensure that patients not benefiting from the expensive critical care setting are transferred to more supportive and less costly settings; nonbeneficial or harmful imaging, laboratory, specialty consultation, and procedures are avoided, and patients are discharged sooner and more safely.[4-8] As a consequence of better family support, care coordination, and home care and hospice referrals, patients are able to remain in their homes after hospital discharge, and costly and preventable hospitalizations, readmissions, and emergency department visits are avoided. Finally, when patients require hospitalization, the availability of palliative care teams means that more hospital admissions go directly to the palliative care service instead of high-critical-care or step-down beds. Studies from Europe[9,10] and the United States[4,7,11-23] suggest that the ability of palliative care teams to help patients avoid hospitalization can be substantial.

Although data on the exact savings provided by palliative care to the healthcare system are not yet available, available research allows reasonable estimates to be made. To date, 12 studies of varying quality and size have examined the impact of palliative care teams on hospital costs[4,7,13,15,24-29] or charges,[30-32] and all but one[29] revealed significant cost savings favoring palliative care. If data from the largest and highest-quality study are used,[4] the average per-patient per-admission net cost saved by hospital palliative care consultation is estimated to be $2,659. As of 2011, 60% of U.S. hospitals with 50 or more beds report having a palliative care team[33,34] and care for approximately 1.5% of all discharges. Given current penetration rates, palliative care is estimated to save $1.2 billion per year in hospital costs under the current services penetration (1.5% of hospital discharges at U.S. hospitals). This figure, however, represents only a fraction of potential savings. If we assume that the vast majority of the 2% of U.S. hospital deaths plus the approximately 4% of patients who are discharged alive with serious illness could benefit from palliative care services, palliative care teams should be caring for approximately 6% of all hospital admissions. If palliative care teams were fully implemented across all U.S. hospitals (i.e., if capacity were expanded to meet the needs of 6% of hospital discharges at 90% of all U.S. hospitals with more than 50 beds), the estimated savings would increase to approximately $4 billion per year.[4,5,35]

In order to bring palliative care to scale in the United States and achieve the steps outlined above, several steps need to be undertaken. These steps include developing appropriate quality measures and assessment, addressing variability in access by geographic and other characteristics, creating an adequate workforce and workforce pipeline to fully staff palliative care teams to meet the needs of patients and their families, enhancing the research evidence base in order to guide high-quality clinical care, and educating the public on the needs and benefits of palliative care.[4,5,35]

Palliative Care Quality

Assessment of palliative care quality and, hence, ensuring that patients and families receive the care that they deserve are currently limited by the lack of an appropriate evidence base.[36] Although investigators in the United States, Canada, Europe, and Australia are investing in and developing outcomes measures for quality improvement and public reporting,[37,38] most measures that currently exist are confined to structures and processes. At present, structure and process measures have been developed by three groups: the National Quality Forum (NQF), the Center to Advance Palliative Care (CAPC), and the Veterans Administration (VA). The NQF Framework and Preferred Practices for Palliative Care[39] includes a number of structure and process measures that are associated with the core elements of palliative care, although their correlation with relevant clinical and family outcomes (symptom burden, caregiver burden, satisfaction, transitions, spiritual distress) are not yet known. Building on the NQF process, Weissman and colleagues[40-43] developed a series of consensus guidelines on structure and process measures for hospital palliative care teams that have been endorsed and published by CAPC. Like the NQF measures, they have been neither field-tested nor validated against patient-level and efficiency outcomes. The VA has developed measures using caregiver postdeath interviews that evaluate communication; emotional and spiritual support; pain management and personal care needs; and chart-based measures that examine the presence of a palliative care consult, chaplain visit, and social work visit and the frequency of bereavement contact with the family after the veteran's death.[44,45]

Several quality initiatives are in development, with publication of new measures expected by late 2011 or 2012. CAPC launched a palliative care program registry (https://registry.capc.org) in 2009[46] for voluntarily reporting on palliative care structure and process measures derived from the NQF Framework and Preferred Practices.[47] Although data from the registry are not currently publicly available, they are promised in 2012, assuming there are enough registrants to allow valid comparison across hospitals. These data will be used to establish palliative care program norms and to assist in programmatic development and quality improvement efforts. NQF is currently reviewing a limited number of quality measures for palliative care, and a small set of endorsed measures should be available in late 2011.[48] Finally, the Joint Commission, which accredits most hospitals in the United States, has created and field-tested a voluntary certificate program derived from the NQF Framework for palliative care,[39] which was released in July of 2011.[49] It is anticipated that data from this certification program will lead to the development of standardized core performance measures. Despite these efforts, additional work to gather data on more comprehensive and extensive standardized empirical quality metrics that can be used for either internal or external quality-reporting and pay-for-performance methods is clearly needed. As with other clinical outcome measures, quality metrics for palliative care should be able to demonstrate a clear link between structure and process and the relevant clinical and patient-centered outcomes, and the measures should represent areas that providers can improve.

Palliative Care Access

Until recently, palliative care services were typically available in only a few scattered academic medical centers.[48] Today, however, palliative care programs are found in hospitals throughout the United States, with more than 60% of U.S. hospitals with at least 50 beds and 80% of hospitals with more than 300 beds reported having a palliative care team—an increase of 134% from 2000.[33,50] Like many aspects of healthcare, access to palliative care is highly variable across the country.

For-profit, southern U.S., and small and safety-net hospitals (fewer than 100 beds) are less likely to report hospital palliative care teams[34,51] compared with not-for-profit hospitals, hospitals outside the South, and larger hospitals. Even in settings in which a palliative care team is available, there is a great deal of variability in the services to which patients have access, ranging, for example, from a half-time nurse to a full interdisciplinary palliative care team.[52] Finally, the presence of a palliative care program does not necessarily equate with access. At most U.S. hospitals, access to palliative care is through referral from the patient's treating physician, which, in itself, is highly variable. Physicians' individual practice patterns, awareness and knowledge of palliative care, and training all influence the likelihood of palliative care teams receiving patient referrals. Universal patient screening for the need for palliative care carried out upon hospital admission could improve access to palliative care by promoting and standardizing early recognition and intervention.[53]

Palliative Care Workforce

An inadequate medical and nursing workforce with expertise in palliative care is an additional barrier to universal access to palliative care. A report commissioned by the Health Resources and Services Administration (HRSA) in 2002 projected significant shortfalls in the nation's number of palliative medicine specialists[54] and called for (1) a policy focused on increased education and training in palliative medicine across all clinical specialties serving patients with serious illness, (2) expanded funding and reimbursement to attract young physicians into the field, and (3) examination of the appropriate role of nonphysician professionals in strengthening access to palliative care across healthcare settings. Another workforce study commissioned by the American Academy of Hospice and Palliative Medicine in 2010 conservatively estimated a shortfall of at least 2,787 full-time—or, given the frequency of part-time participation in the field, approximately 6,000 palliative medicine physicians.[55] This estimate did not factor in the as yet unmet need for access to outpatient specialist-level palliative care. Because the time- and communication-intensive nature of palliative care precludes standard productivity measures based on the volume of patients seen, part of the difficulty in expanding workforce capacity is the lack of appropriate and standardized productivity and compensation models for palliative care physician and nurse practitioner services in both inpatient and outpatient settings.

A continuing barrier to ensuring an adequate physician palliative care workforce is the cap on Medicare-funded graduate medical education (GME) slots in U.S. teaching hospitals.[56,57] Since the Balanced Budget Act of 1997, the total number of Medicare-funded GME training slots (both residency and fellowship) has been frozen at about 80,000.[57,58] Aside from sleep medicine, palliative medicine is the only specialty approved by the American Board of Medical Specialties since 1997 and, as such, has no existing and established Medicare-funded GME slots. At present, the distribution of GME slots is entirely within the purview of each teaching hospital and is not federally mandated. Thus, palliative medicine must either secure vacant GME slots (unavailable at the leading teaching hospitals) or convince such hospitals to reallocate funded slots from long-standing and preexisting training programs (a typically impossible task). As a result, specialty training in palliative medicine is largely dependent on private-sector philanthropy. In recognition of the need for data to inform federal training priorities, the August 2010 U.S. Senate Appropriations Committee report for the departments of Labor, Health and Human Services, and Education for FY 2011 included language in its Health Professions Workforce Information and Analysis section calling for HRSA-sponsored studies on the adequacy of the palliative care workforce.

Palliative Care Research

Investment in research is critically needed to guide clinical care and to develop and test promising delivery models in a range of patient populations and settings. Even though the U.S. population is aging and persons with serious illness account for the bulk of healthcare spending,[59] less than 0.01% of National Institutes of Health (NIH) extramural research grants between 2003 and 2005 funded palliative care–related research.[60] With rare exceptions,[61] private-sector philanthropy rarely invests in research, thereby placing additional pressure on federal funding sources to fill the gaps. Reflecting awareness of this problem, the August 2010 U.S. Senate Appropriations Committee report for the departments of Labor, Health and Human Services, and Education for FY 2011, in its section on the National Institutes of Health, called for a transinstitute strategy aimed at increasing funding for palliative care research.

Palliative Care Public Education and Awareness

A major barrier to the continued growth of palliative care is the misperception that palliative care is synonymous with hospice, "end-of-life care," care of the dying, or the alternative to curative or life-prolonging treatments, particularly in the minds of healthcare professionals and policy makers. This unfortunate professional misunderstanding inhibits access to palliative care early in the course of illness, when patients and families can benefit greatly from the services palliative care provides. As more fully described in chapter 6, palliative care is appropriate at the point of diagnosis of a serious illness and provides an extra layer of support for patients and families. It is available to patients who continue to benefit from curative or life-prolonging treatments. Furthermore, focusing on the "end of life" or care of the dying is politically problematic. Whereas explanations of humans' long-standing fear of death have ranged from evolutionary to societal,[62-65] the practical result is that efforts to focus healthcare reform on "end-of-life care" have met with resistance and have been relatively ineffective.[66]

A national public education campaign to increase public and professional awareness about palliative care is critically needed and supported by recent public opinion research funded by the CAPC and the American Cancer Society.[67] In a sample of 800 Americans (oversampled for those over age 65 years), only 8% of respondents reported being familiar or very familiar with the term "palliative care."[67] However, when read a definition of palliative care and the services that palliative care teams provide, 92% of respondents reported that they would want palliative care for themselves or their loved ones in the setting of a serious illness, 92% reported that palliative care services should be made available at all hospitals for patients with serious illness and their families, and 80% stated that palliative care should be fully covered by Medicare.[67] A national public awareness campaign would define palliative care as appropriate care for persons with serious illness throughout the course of their disease, would encourage patients and families to seek high-quality palliative care early in the course of illness, and would educate healthcare professionals as to the appropriate role of palliative care in the care of their patients. This campaign, similar to initiatives centered on smoking cessation and childhood obesity, would considerably facilitate enhanced access to palliative care.

Palliative Care and the Affordable Care Act of 2010: A Potential Opportunity

Although many provisions related to access to quality palliative care were ultimately removed from the original health reform bills, including the S.1150 Advance Care Planning and Compassionate Care Act[68] and the Life Sustaining Treatment Preference Act,[69] several provisions relevant to palliative care remain. Although not mandated in the Affordable Care Act, the new law does enable the integration and participation of palliative care teams as a component of the new delivery and payment models, such as accountable care organizations (ACOs), patient-centered medical homes (PCMHs, also known as Health Homes), and the bundling of payments for a single episode of healthcare. Each of these models aims to (1) improve quality and control cost for high-need patient populations by focusing on patient-centered, goal-driven, and intensive care coordination; (2) identify and treat problems before crises prompt preventable emergency department visits or hospitalizations; and (3) shift provider incentives from fee-for-service drivers of quantity to payment based on quality. Despite the potential for palliative care to improve the ability of new delivery and payment models to improve quality and reduce cost, there is as yet no mandate for their inclusion and no certainty about the likelihood of their integration in the future.

Conclusions

The evolution and growth of palliative care in the United Sates have resulted from the combined investments of both public and private sectors. The new delivery and payment models encouraged by the Affordable Care Act and aimed at a high-risk, high-need target population have the potential to strengthen palliative care capacity in the acute, postacute, and long-term care settings for seriously ill patients. Substantial private-sector contributions exceeding $300 million in the past 25 years have created the new field of palliative care and are reflected in the growth of hospital palliative care services, education and training for health professionals, and formal recognition of subspecialty status for physicians and nurses. Major healthcare organizations, such as the American Hospital Association's annual Circle of Life Awards for quality palliative care programs, the Joint Commission's new Certification Program in Palliative Care, and the American Cancer Society's Pathfinder in Palliative Care Award, have also made sustained and influential commitments to advancing access to quality palliative care for the seriously ill. Small pilot palliative care programs in commercial and integrated health plans have experimented with creative payment models resulting in better value (i.e., higher quality and lower costs).[70,71] Public-sector initiatives as outlined above are now necessary in order to bring palliative care innovation to scale in the United States and to ensure value in healthcare for the millions of Americans living with serious illness and their families.

References

1. Henry J. Kaiser Family Foundation. Trends in health care costs and spending. No. 7692-02, March 2009. http://www.kff.org/insurance/upload/7692_02.pdf. Accessed September 9, 2011.

2. Dartmouth Atlas of Health Care. http://www.dartmouthatlas.org/. Accessed September 9, 2011.

3. Kelley AS, Ettner SL, Morrison RS, Du Q, Wenger NS, Sarkisian CA. Determinants of medical expenditures in the last 6 months of life. *Annals of Internal Medicine.* 2011;154(4):235-242.

4. Morrison RS, Penrod JD, Cassel JB, et al. Cost savings associated with US hospital palliative care consultation programs. *Archives of Internal Medicine.* 2008;168(16):1783-1790.

5. Siu AL, Spragens LH, Inouye SK, Morrison RS, Leff B. The ironic business case for chronic care in the acute care setting. *Health Affairs (Millwood).* 2009;28(1):113-125.

6. Brody AA, Ciemins E, Newman J, Harrington C. The effects of an inpatient palliative care team on discharge disposition. *Journal of Palliative Medicine.* 2010;13(5):541-548.

7. Temel JS, Greer JA, Muzikansky A, et al. Early palliative care for patients with metastatic non-small-cell lung cancer. *New England Journal of Medicine.* 2010;363(8):733-742.

8. Smith AK, Schonberg MA, Fisher J, et al. Emergency department experiences of acutely symptomatic patients with terminal illness and their family caregivers. *Journal of Pain and Symptom Management.* 2010;39(6):972-981.

9. Higginson IJ, Finlay I, Goodwin DM, et al. Do hospital-based palliative teams improve care for patients or families at the end of life? *Journal of Pain and Symptom Management.* 2002;23(2):96-106.

10. Jordhøy MS, Fayers P, Saltnes T, Ahlner-Elmqvist M, Jannert M, Kaasa S. A palliative-care intervention and death at home: a cluster randomised trial. *Lancet.* 2000;356(9233):888-893.

11. Bakitas M, Lyons KD, Hegel MT, et al. Effects of a palliative care intervention on clinical outcomes in patients with advanced cancer: the project ENABLE II randomized controlled trial. *JAMA: Journal of the American Medical Association.* 2009;302(7):741-749.

12. Back AL, Li YF, Sales AE. Impact of palliative care case management on resource use by patients dying of cancer at a Veterans Affairs medical center. *Journal of Palliative Medicine.* 2005;8(1):26-35.

13. Smith TJ, Coyne P, Cassel B, Penberthy L, Hopson A, Hager MA. A high-volume specialist palliative care unit and team may reduce in-hospital end-of-life care costs. *Journal of Palliative Medicine.* 2003;6(5):699-705.

14. Elsayem A, Swint K, Fisch MJ, et al. Palliative care inpatient service in a comprehensive cancer center: clinical and financial outcomes. *Journal of Clinical Oncology.* 2004;22(10):2008-2014.

15. Penrod JD, Deb P, Luhrs C, et al. Cost and utilization outcomes of patients receiving hospital-based palliative care consultation. *Journal of Palliative Medicine.* 2006;9(4):855-860.

16. Anderson GM, Horvath J. *Chronic conditions: making the case for ongoing care.* Baltimore: Johns Hopkins University; 2002.

17. Zhang B, Wright AA, Huskamp HA, et al. Health care costs in the last week of life: associations with end-of-life conversations. *Archives of Internal Medicine.* 2009;169(5):480-488.

18. Wright AA, Zhang B, Ray A, et al. Associations between end-of-life discussions, patient mental health, medical care near death, and caregiver bereavement adjustment. *JAMA: Journal of the American Medical Association.* 2008;300(14):1665-1673.

19. Brumley R, Enguidanos S, Jamison P, et al. Increased satisfaction with care and lower costs: results of a randomized trial of in-home palliative care. *Journal of the American Geriatrics Society.* 2007;55(7):993-1000.

20. Harding R, Gomes B, Foley KM, Higginson IJ. Research priorities in health economics and funding for palliative care: views of an international think tank. *Journal of Pain and Symptom Management.* 2009;38(1):11-14.

21. Smith TJ, Cassel JB. Cost and non-clinical outcomes of palliative care. *Journal of Pain and Symptom Management.* 2009;38(1):32-44.

22. Gomes B, Harding R, Foley KM, Higginson IJ. Optimal approaches to the health economics of palliative care: report of an international think tank. *Journal of Pain and Symptom Management.* 2009;38(1):4-10.

23. Taylor DH,Jr, Ostermann J, Van Houtven CH, Tulsky JA, Steinhauser K. What length of hospice use maximizes reduction in medical expenditures near death in the US Medicare program? *Social Science and Medicine.* 2007;65(7):1466-1478.

24. Penrod JD, Deb P, Dellenbaugh C, et al. Hospital-based palliative care consultation: effects on hospital cost. *Journal of Palliative Medicine.* 2010;13(8):973-979.

25. Morrison RS, Dietrich J, Ladwig S, et al. Palliative care consultation teams cut hospital costs for Medicaid beneficiaries. *Health Affairs (Millwood).* 2011;30(3):454-463.

26. Ciemins EL, Blum L, Nunley M, Lasher A, Newman JM. The economic and clinical impact of an inpatient palliative care consultation service: a multifaceted approach. *Journal of Palliative Medicine.* 2007;10(6):1347-1355.

27. Hanson LC, Usher B, Spragens L, Bernard S. Clinical and economic impact of palliative care consultation. *Journal of Pain and Symptom Management.* 2008;35(4):340-346.

28. Twaddle ML, Maxwell TL, Cassel JB, et al. Palliative care benchmarks from academic medical centers. *Journal of Palliative Medicine.* 2007;10(1):86-98.

29. Gade G, Venohr I, Conner D, et al. Impact of an inpatient palliative care team: a randomized control trial. *Journal of Palliative Medicine.* 2008;11(2):180-190.

30. O'Mahony S, Blank AE, Zallman L, Selwyn PA. The benefits of a hospital-based inpatient palliative care consultation service: preliminary outcome data. *Journal of Palliative Medicine.* 2005;8(5):1033-1039.

31. Cowan JD. Hospital charges for a community inpatient palliative care program. *American Journal of Hospice and Palliative Medicine.* 2004;21(3):177-190.

31. Bendaly EA, Groves J, Juliar B, Gramelspacher GP. Financial impact of palliative care consultation in a public hospital. *Journal of Palliative Medicine.* 2008;11(10):1304-1308.

33. Goldsmith B, Dietrich J, Du Q, Morrison RS. Variability in access to hospital palliative care in the United States. *Journal of Palliative Medicine.* 2008;11(8):1094-1102.

34. Center to Advance Palliative Care. Analysis of US hospital palliative care programs: 2010 snapshot. http://www.capc.org/news-and-events/releases/analysis-of-us-hospital-palliative-care-programs-2010-snapshot.pdf/file_view. Accessed September 9, 2011.

35. Morrison RS, Meier DE, Carlson M. Palliative care, access, quality, and costs. In: Yong PL, Saunders RS, Olsen L, eds. *The healthcare imperative: lowering costs and improving outcomes.* Washington, DC: National Academies Press; 2011:498-503.

36. Morrison RS, Siu AL, Leipzig RM, Cassel CK, Meier DE. The hard task of improving the quality of care at the end of life. *Archives of Internal Medicine*. 2000;160(6):743-747.

37. Currow DC, Eagar K, Aoun S, Fildes D, Yates P, Kristjanson LJ. Is it feasible and desirable to collect voluntarily quality and outcome data nationally in palliative oncology care? *Journal of Clinical Oncology*. 2008;26(23):3853-3859.

38. Anderson GF, Squires DA. Measuring the U.S. health care system: a cross-national comparison. *Issue Brief (Commonwealth Fund)*. 2010;90:1-10.

39. National Quality Forum (NQF). National framework and preferred practices for palliative and hospice care quality. http://www.qualityforum.org/Projects/n-r/ Palliative_and_Hospice_Care_Framework/Palliative_Hospice_Care_Framework_ and_Practices.aspx. Accessed August 30, 2011.

40. Weissman DE, Meier DE, Spragens LH. Center to Advance Palliative Care palliative care consultation service metrics: consensus recommendations. *Journal of Palliative Medicine*. 2008;11(10):1294-1298.

41. Weissman DE, Meier DE. Operational features for hospital palliative care programs: consensus recommendations. *Journal of Palliative Medicine*. 2008;11(9):1189-1194.

42. Weissman DE, Meier DE. Center to Advance Palliative Care inpatient unit operational metrics: consensus recommendations. *Journal of Palliative Medicine*. 2009;12(1):21-25.

43. Weissman DE, Morrison RS, Meier DE. Center to Advance Palliative Care palliative care clinical care and customer satisfaction metrics consensus recommendations. *Journal of Palliative Medicine*. 2010;13(2):179-84.

44. Casarett D, Shreve S, Luhrs C, et al. Measuring families' perceptions of care across a health care system: preliminary experience with the family assessment of treatment at end of life short form (FATE-S). *Journal of Pain and Symptom Management*. 2010;40(6):801-809.

45. Lu H, Trancik E, Bailey FA, et al. Families' perceptions of end-of-life care in Veterans Affairs versus non-Veterans Affairs facilities. *Journal of Palliative Medicine*. 2010;13(8):991-996.

46. Center to Advance Palliative Care. National palliative care registry. https://registry. capc.org/Default.aspx. Accessed September 9, 2011.

47. National Quality Forum (NQF). National voluntary consensus standards for palliative care and end-of-life care. http://www.qualityforum.org/Projects/n-r/

Palliative_Care_and_End-of-Life_Care/Palliative_Care_and_End-of-Life_Care.
aspx. Accessed September 9, 2011.

48. National Consensus Project for Quality Palliative Care. *Clinical practice guidelines for quality palliative care.* New York: National Consensus Project for Quality Palliative Care; 2004.

49. Joint Commission. Advanced certification for palliative care programs: disease specific certification. http://www.jointcommission.org/certification/palliative_care. aspx. Accessed August 30, 2011.

50. American Hospital Association. *AHA hospital statistics.* Chicago: Health Forum; 2008.

51. Center to Advance Palliative Care. America's care of serious illness: a state-by-state report card on access to palliative care in our nation's hospitals. http://www.capc. org/reportcard/. Accessed September 9, 2011.

52. Medicare Payment Advisory Commission (MedPAC), Report to the Congress: Medicare payment policies, March 2010: p. 148. http://www.medpac.gov/ documents/Mar10_EntireReport.pdf. Accessed September 13, 2011.

53. Weissman DE, Meier DE. Identifying patients in need of a palliative care assessment in the hospital setting: a consensus report from the Center to Advance Palliative Care. *Journal of Palliative Medicine.* 2011;14(1):17-23.

54. Cowan BP, Salsberg E. *The supply, demand, and use of palliative care physicians in the United States.* Rensselaer, NY: Center for Health Workforce Studies, School of Public Health, SUNY Albany; 2002.

55. Lupu D, American Academy of Hospice and Palliative Medicine Workforce Task Force. Estimate of current hospice and palliative medicine physician workforce shortage. *Journal of Pain and Symptom Management.* 2010;40(6):899-911.

56. American Association of Medical Colleges. Recent studies and reports on physician shortages in the U.S. https://www.aamc.org/initiatives/workforce/. Accessed September 13, 2011.

57. Salsberg E, Rockey PH, Rivers KL, Brotherton SE, Jackson GR. US residency training before and after the 1997 balanced budget act. *JAMA: Journal of the American Medical Association.* 2008;300(10):1174-1180.

58. Landers SJ. Bill would raise cap on Medicare-funded residency slots. *American Medical News,* May 28, 2009. http://www.ama-assn.org/amednews/2009/05/25/ prse0528.htm. Accessed September 9, 2011.

59. The Lewin Group. *Individuals living in the community with chronic conditions and functional limitations: a closer look.* Washington, DC: Office of the Assistant Secretary for Planning and Evaluation, US Department of Health and Human Services; 2010. http://aspe.hhs.gov/daltcp/reports/2010/closerlook.pdf. Accessed September 13, 2011.

60. Gelfman LP, Morrison RS. Research funding for palliative medicine. *Journal of Palliative Medicine.* 2008;11(1):36-43.

61. National Palliative Care Research Center. http://www.npcrc.org/. Accessed September 9, 2011.

62. Darwin C. *The origin of the species by means of natural selection of the preservation of favoured races in the struggle for life.* New York: Signet Classic; 2003.

63. Becker E. *The denial of death.* New York: Free Press; 1973:314.

64. Hofmann JC, Wenger NS, Davis RB, et al. Patient preferences for communication with physicians about end-of-life decisions: SUPPORT investigators: study to understand prognoses and preference for outcomes and risks of treatment. *Annals of Internal Medicine.* 1997;127(1):1-12.

65. O'Gorman SM. Death and dying in contemporary society: an evaluation of current attitudes and the rituals associated with death and dying and their relevance to recent understandings of health and healing. *Journal of Advanced Nursing.* 1998;27(6):1127-1135.

66. Grassley HJ. Government shouldn't "decide when to pull the plug on grandma." *Iowa Independent.* August 12, 2009. http://iowaindependent.com/18456/grassley-government-shouldnt-decide-when-to-pull-the-plug-on-grandma. Accessed September 9, 2011.

67. Center to Advance Palliative Care. 2011 public opinion research on palliative care: a report based on research by public opinion strategies. http://www.capc.org/tools-for-palliative-care-programs/marketing/public-opinion-research/2011-public-opinion-research-on-palliative-care.pdf. Accessed August 26, 2011.

68. Senator John Rockefeller. Advance Planning and Compassionate Care Act of 2009. Vol. S. 1150, No. 111th.

69. Rep. Earl Blumenauer. Life Sustaining Treatment Preferences Act of 2009. Vol. H.R. 1898, No. 111th.

70. Krakauer R, Spettell CM, Reisman L, Wade MJ. Opportunities to improve the quality of care for advanced illness. *Health Affairs (Millwood).* 2009;28(5):1357-1359.

71. Spettell CM, Rawlins WS, Krakauer R, et al. A comprehensive case
     management program to improve palliative care. *Journal of Palliative Medicine*.
     2009;12(9):827-832.

Section V

What's Next?

sixteen

Call to Action: What Needs to Change to Improve Care and Allow Sustainability

—Jeff Thompson, MD,
and Patrick Fry

IT'S CLEAR THAT huge gaps separate the work of the pioneers featured in this book from current healthcare practice. Major changes are needed if we are to follow the lead of these innovators and truly focus our efforts on the well-being of seriously ill patients and their families. As they are doing, we must work much harder to hear the patient's voice at critical times in the cycle of illness, when it may be especially vulnerable and weak.

But our task goes far beyond simply listening. We must help patients and their families to become engaged in their own care. This demands of us that we commit the time and effort to make solid plans together, as providers and patients, before the crises happen. We must all realize that if we don't make these decisions soon enough, someone else, often a family member, sometimes a caregiver, will be forced to carry the terrible weight of making these decisions for us.

231

Along with the right to determine one's own care comes the responsibility to organize it ahead of time so that this task is not thrust upon those who care for us and about us.

Yet families themselves cannot evade responsibility. They need to be fully engaged in this process and urge all their members to have open discussions, to consider multiple options, and to be mutually supportive in both the conversation and the carrying out of their loved ones' wishes. In this engagement lies a tremendous opportunity to improve our care by focusing together on the patient's best interests and to help ensure the well-being of the family into the future.

Frankly, we healthcare providers bear important responsibilities that we have not been fulfilling. Of course, we can't force patients to develop advanced care plans or compel doctors to complete Physician Orders for Life-Sustaining Treatment (POLST). However, we can and must structure an environment where those things happen naturally. Our accountability as healthcare leaders extends far beyond the walls of our hospitals and indeed beyond the boundaries of our integrated systems. It must extend even further, into our communities and into our culture at large.

We should be responsible for creating smooth, efficient, and understandable opportunities for dialogue and planning not only in the healthcare setting but also with community and religious groups. This kind of communication needs to become the norm across our country. As our population ages, we need to help the dialogue evolve into a common conversation that provides broad and deep support to patients and families so that they can arrive at consensus well before a crisis. And we need to develop the structures to communicate their decisions to all potential points of care and then to ensure that their wishes are followed. This must become the community standard of care not just within innovative centers but everywhere.

Our mission and, thus, our primary responsibility are clear. In short, we must create a system that places the well-being of the patient above the interests of the system. In today's fee-for-service environment, when patients choose less aggressive approaches, revenues may decrease, particularly for hospitals.

Our organizations must anticipate that and account for it by attending to our own costs. In addition, we must take the lead in developing alternative reimbursement structures that align the incentives of all clinicians to provide care of the greatest value. We will have to assume financial risk to make this happen, but that will serve to push us to fulfill the value proposition.

Other tools will be important in this work. Staff education across all segments of our delivery system will help clinicians to deliver thoughtful and understandable information to help guide and engage patients and their families. This should be viewed as an integral part of today's growing emphasis on improved information systems, as our organizations broaden their networks of electronic records to share data widely and securely across specialties, geography, and even the boundaries among multiple systems. To achieve this, collaboration will be required among healthcare organizations, their surrounding communities, and government.

As health systems become more accountable for wise and responsible communication, the same will be required of our legislative bodies. Open dialogue and collaboration can help us develop new laws and regulations that foster patient and family well-being. State and federal legislators should actively engage with healthcare providers and their communities in order to understand the struggles of patients and families as they come to terms with serious illness. We need legislators and the administration to focus not only on the cries of the media and the needs of the economy but also on the well-being of patients and their families.

Large employers and coalitions also have an important stake in the health and well-being of their employees and of their communities. From an economic standpoint, this involves lowering their state and federal tax burdens and decreasing cost shifting from the federal side to employer-based programs. But there are more important benefits. A growing number of employees will become caregivers of their aging parents, creating an ever-increasing burden in the workplace. Employer-community collaboration will improve the tone of the discussion and the distribution of information and, more importantly, will lower stress and improve stability among employees.

Finally, we must work together to counter the toxic rhetoric that sometimes impedes progress in improving care of the seriously ill. People should be held accountable for statements made for partisan reasons, no matter which side they come from. The well-being of patients and communities is not served by rhetoric that promotes fear. We must acknowledge the natural fears associated with serious illness, for that is part of the human condition. But we must also propose real solutions to real problems, even in cases where curing is not possible and only caring helps. This is the way toward the kind of authentic hope that triumphs over fear. This is what seriously ill patients and their families need most. Regardless of the stage of their illness, we must help people to the greatest extent possible to live comfortable, happy, and independent lives.

Our cause is noble, and if we work together, the potential for success is high. But we need to remember that this kind of change doesn't happen on its own. It takes dedicated individuals, from multiple venues, over a sustained span of time to achieve the outcomes we seek. This is not simply a project. It is a new approach to the health and well-being of the most vulnerable citizens in our communities. Our patients and their families must have a voice in their care, but more than that, we need to help them take action. Healthcare has to be responsible for providing a better environment for patients and, beyond that, for our staff to deliver this very personal level of care. In this way we will create positive and lasting change in the culture of our care and even in the values of our society.

We will be successful to the extent that, across the healthcare environment, we work with patients and families, religious groups, schools, and service organizations to build a system that transcends our current conception of health and illness. Ideally, we would formulate a broad plan for community health and well-being spanning all ages, throughout all phases of life. By doing so, we would strengthen the fabric of our communities and, in turn, the health of our country.

Every great journey begins with a few small steps in the right direction. The authors of the chapters in this book describe innovative approaches in various stages of development and in diverse locations, approaches that are beginning to show the way toward a new kind of care that gives patients a more full voice, a care that engages families and communities. As a fortunate consequence, this approach is also less costly. Interventions like this are not common in healthcare. We need to find ways to support their development and dissemination, so all people, whether they're healthy or ill, can gain the benefits.

Patrick Fry joined Sutter Health in 1982 as an administrative resident at Sutter General Hospital in Sacramento. Over the years he held increasingly responsible administrative positions—at both the local affiliate level and the region level—with responsibilities covering the breadth of Sutter Health's services.

After serving as regional president for Sutter Health's affiliates in the greater Sacramento region, Mr. Fry became president of the organization's eastern operations. He later assumed leadership of Sutter Health's Western Division and in 2000 became Sutter Health's second-in-command, serving as chief operating officer and executive vice president. In 2005, Mr. Fry became president and CEO of the not-for-profit healthcare organization.

The California Hospitals Association elected Mr. Fry board of trustees chair for 2010. His educational background includes a bachelor's degree in public health administration from the University of California, Davis, and a master's degree in health services administration from George Washington University in Washington, DC. He is a member of the American College of Health Care Executives (ACHE), the Medical Group Management Association (MGMA), and the Leadership Institute.

About Gundersen Health System

HEADQUARTERED IN LA CROSSE, Wis., Gundersen Health System is a comprehensive healthcare network with a hospital and clinics throughout Wisconsin, Minnesota, and Iowa. Gundersen is a major tertiary teaching hospital, providing a broad range of emergency, specialty, and primary care services.

As one of the nation's largest multi-specialty group medical practices, Gundersen is comprised of more than 700 medical, dental and associate staff, and supported by a staff of more than 5,500. The Health System has been consistently ranked in the upper 5% of hospitals in the country by independent healthcare ratings organizations.

In addition, Gundersen is known for their work to improve care at the end of life and has two internationally recognized programs on advance care planning: Respecting Choices and If I Only Knew. Respecting Choices has been implemented by more than 60 organizations or groups in the United States, is being implemented country-wide in Australia and Singapore, and is being tested in Germany, Spain and Canada.

Learn more at www.gundluth.org

236